FROM GARRISON TO GARDEN VOL.1 - BOOTS ON THE GROUND

Untold stories from the inner city

Moira Morgan

Mo Morgan Books - momorganbooks@gmail.com

*This book is dedicated to
Mummy, Daddy and Popsie, the lessons you
taught us were well learned, the greatest of which
has been Unconditional Love for ALL.*

You have your Jamaica and I have mine......

You have your Jamaica with all its dilemmas,
I have my Jamaica with all its beauty.

You have your Jamaica with all its conflicts that rage there
I have my Jamaica with all the dreams that live there

You have your Jamaica and you accept it,
I have my Jamaica and I accept nothing less than peace, love and unity

Your Jamaica is a political knot which the years attempt to untie.
My Jamaica is made up of hills which rise with great presence and magnificence towards the deep blue sky.

Your Jamaica is an international problem beset with the shadows of night
My Jamaica is made up of silent and mysterious valleys, whose slopes gather together the sounds of bells and the tinkling of streams, the running of the rivers and the roaring of the sea.

Your Jamaica is a tilting ground where 'Dons' from the West struggle with others from the South.
My Jamaica is a winged prayer which hovers on the morning with the mists and flies away at evening with the setting of the sun.

Your Jamaica is a chessboard set between religious and political leaders
My Jamaica is a temple which I visit within my spirit when my eyes weary of the face of this civilisation which advances on greed.

Your Jamaica thrives on violence, greed and guns
My Jamaica is a distant memory, an ardent desire and a nostalgic word whispered in the ear of the Universe.

Your Jamaica is a land of 'garrisons' and 'parties', speeches and disputes
My Jamaica is made up of children who strive to climb the rocks of opposition and run with the streams of life.

Your Jamaica is no more than deceit and hypocrisy concealed by mannerisms and playacting.

My Jamaica is simple naked truth as it's people accept their inborn knowledge in the mysteries of life, the simplicity of truth and love.

And, what of the children of your Jamaica,
They are those who are unaware of famine unless it robs their pocket.
And if they meet a hungry spirit they will laugh at him and avoid him, treating him as of no worth.

Who among them would represent the power of Jamaica's hills, the nobility of their heights, the crystal of their waters, the fragrances of their air?
Who among them could say 'When I die, I shall have left my country slightly better than it was at my birth'.

Who would dare to say 'Indeed my life was a drop of blood in the veins of Jamaica or a smile on its lips'.
Do they deign to believe that when they pray, the upper air absorbs their shadows of hate, indifference, destruction, death and corruption?

Well let me show you the children of my Jamaica...........
They are those who trusting in God are the tillers of soil,
They are those men who harvest the crops, whose families gather it up in armfuls.

They are those who sell by the roadside their crops and their wares
Who remember a time when my Jamaica was so.
Their pride is in compassion, peace and the triumph of good,
Their ethics, morals and love overriding any need for power

They are those whose values and lives are tied to the seasons and to nurturing each other
To whom learning is a valued joy unlimited.
They are those who stay and they try, and try, and try, and try
....

ADAPTED FROM KHALIL GIBRAN'S 'YOU HAVE YOUR LEBANON
AND I HAVE MINE'
MOIRA MORGAN 27TH AUGUST 2004

CONTENTS

Title Page   1

Dedication   3

Epigraph   4

Foreword   9

Introduction   15

Preface   21

Jamaica timeline   23

Acknowledgements   27

How it all began   29

foundation   31

1977 - 1998   36

Cricket   39

Hellshire Blessings   45

1999 to 2001 Short Trips   53

New York   60

Meeting New Folk   62

2002   69

Zinc   70

Teacher   78

Just a little hike Blue Mountain   81

Marching Band   86

Unity Summer Camp	89
Unity Summer Camp Day trip	91
Unity Summer Camp - The last week	93
2003	95
Learning to duck	96
Kings House	104
Generosity	106
Coming together	110
Murphy's Law	114
Summer Camp	122
Shoe Boxes	126
Elders Treat	131
2004	135
progress	136
Mi did a warn yuh!	138
Stone Soup	144
Iris	149
Ms Marva	153
From Garrison to Garden Vol. 2 - Time for Sanctuary	157
Time to Move	158
About The Author	161
Praise For Author	163
From Garrison to Garden	165

FOREWORD

In perusing this book, one senses that it was important to the author to have written this book. It is important to the author to have documented the stories and events that jump from its pages as it will be for its content to be absorbed into the hearts and minds of its readers.

The text captures the raison d'etre for the high regard that many persons, across disciplines, across classes, and across borders have had for Mrs Morgan and her work, as she has toiled, in the vineyard of Jamaican community-based social work, at its most visceral level, for so many decades.

The documentation of this work means that she has validated the realities of thousands of children, youths, women and families within the context of a culture of poverty, that is the reality of the urban social landscape in the under-resourced communities of Jamaica and in other developing societies across the globe.

The documentation described in the pages of this single text, is unique in that it demonstrates the inherent simplicity, as well as the complexities of the needs of the Jamaican urban social landscape.

From the complexities involved in navigating garrison politics, and confronting the realities of urban decay and ongoing political exploitation, the author has documented in this text how she along with an army of ordinary well-meaning community members, (characters we know well, are found in every community), systematically confronted the myriad social issues affecting Jamaican children, over three decades from the eighties, across the decade of the nineties and well into the new millennia.

She vividly describes, and more importantly provides working solutions and prescriptions to the socio-cultural and psycho-social reality of the numerous ills facing Jamaican children and youth. As she documents chapter by chapter, myriad issues of community violence, domestic family violence, as well as child abuse, and child neglect, she shares the narratives of children and youths experiencing for example, betrayal trauma of the Barrel Child syndrome, the loneliness of abandonment due to childhood disability and the ever-present painful reality of violence towards women, children and youths in all its forms.

Using these poignant stories, Mrs Morgan has weaved a vivid tapestry of experiences that make up the social fabric of the urban inner city of Kingston Jamaica. This text can prove useful for students, (many of whom are privileged, and have a limited understanding of the lived experiences of their compatriots). The text can also be helpful to practitioners and policy makers, to help them to compile concrete and permanent policy prescriptions for change that many academics and political representatives have been searching for, for decades.

The author's use of Jamaican patois, and its translations, has strengthened the appeal of the text, so that its issues are easily identifiable globally, to those who work to fight poverty, whether in Jamaica and the rest of the Caribbean, Europe, Asia or North America.

This book can provide a useful read, therefore for the student, the policy maker, or interestingly, the young philanthropist, who may have arrived in Jamaica for the first time, wanting to help, wanting to make a change, or to make a difference. The text reveals the other side of Jamaica which like all other counties, has serious social problems. These problems are however often missed by the millions of visitors to our islands in the Caribbean, and more importantly missed by the middle and the upper-class inhabitants of our shores who interact with, work alongside, and rub shoulders with daily, the characters whose lives are documented in the pages of this text.

As an Irish national in Jamaica, she is uniquely placed to document the experiences of the urban poor and uses a kaleidoscope of images to document and portray the unique ways in which the metropolitan north and the migration and other experiences of the average Jamaican as part of the Global south, interface seamlessly from Kingston to London and New York and back. Mrs Morgan describes the daily struggles of persons in a number of intersecting communities within St Andrew South, the epicentre being the Tower Hill and Cockburn Pen communities that occurred between the late eighties, through the nineties, into the first decade of the new millennium, painting an important historical documentation of social life and its changes, at the community level in urban Jamaica.

The text exposes the underbelly of Jamaican culture of those who are poor and in need in Jamaican society, in relation to the realities of inner city community dynamics and poverty that has rarely been documented from a "bottom-up perspective" In doing this she has added to the pool of knowledge of Jamaican community culture, and has built on the road paved by stalwarts such as by professional community social worker, Francis Madden, Social Anthropologist, Barrington Chevannes, and Horace Levy, community activist. She does this in a manner that is useful for teaching social service practitioners and policy makers alike.

This occurs because the reader is helped to understand the issues in terms of the etiology of our social problems at the community levels. The reader is also helped to see how to navigate funding resources efficiently using a "Tun yuh han mek fashion" model (adapt to one's circumstances based on what you have available) that is so familiar to Jamaican social life and lifestyle. In doing this she shows us how one can create opportunities and effective interventions that are replicable across the Jamaica and Caribbean diaspora, and in the counties of the so-called third world, whether in India the Asia-Pacific pacific islands or in the countries of the African continent.

The work therefore cuts across the traditional social work perspectives, using case studies at the micro level, but also assists in helping the reader understand how an effective practitioner has to navigate across systems at the mezzo community-level dynamic of the inner city, and translate that into linkages in the global philanthropic networks to create meaningful change in the lives of those in need.

Using strategies that would only be possible for a feisty, but caring, loved, and lovable Irish woman "from foreign", Mrs Morgan uses a vignette-based narrative style to present a simple but complex tapestry of life in urban Jamaica that needs to be understood if we are to challenge the root cause of Jamaica's social and economic inequities.

Mrs Morgan is to be commended for writing this book. It does not pretend to be a scholarly academic presentation, but It will be able to inform scholars, both researchers and practitioners, because it does present a wealth of data that can be used by those who are serious about understanding the aetiology of the Jamaican persistent poverty, using anecdotal evidence from the authors own experiences. In her own inimitable style, the lived experiences of the participants flow from the authors pen as she performs he sometimes risky task of "mothering the communities in which she worked at the same time gathering data as a participant observer. This is its strength.

The task now is to ensure that its content gets into the hands of practitioners as well as policy makers, so it can be used to create the fire for advocacy and change so desperately needed by the scores of individuals, whose lives she has so sensitively documented in these pages.

I personally would like to use this this opportunity to thank Mrs Morgan who I have known for the past two decades, for the selfless sacrifices she has made to the individuals and communities that she has touched in Jamaica. I wish that this book will create the kind of interest and discussion that will somehow lead to meaningful change for the thousands in similar communities across this country, who are trapped, trapped because there is so much potential, but so many opportunities are beyond the reach of so many.

This book is needed for teaching so that this generation of social workers understand where we were before and still are today.

Failure to listen to the cries of the voices documented in these pages by this daughter of the soil, can only be to the peril of this beautiful vibrant society, a place which a couple millions of us, lovingly and unrepentantly call home.

Claudette Crawford-Brown PhD Child and Family Welfare Consultant, Former Senior Lecturer in Clinical Social Work - University of the West Indies, Mona

May 2020

INTRODUCTION

Across the three volumes of From Garrison to Garden I chart my journey through the inner cities of Kingston Jamaica, telling the stories of some of the people good and not so good along the way, giving an insight into what makes growing and living in the garrison and poor rural communities, so difficult for so many.

Writing these books has been no easy task. I debated long and hard with myself, were these even my stories to tell? Yes, I wanted to chart my journey, but more importantly, the untold stories screamed to be voiced, almost as though saying, "who remembers, or even cares to remember?", "who cares to understand why?"

The stories are told without judgement, not to condone or excuse, but to explain people in their own words and my personal experience of them, who they are or were and to help understand why some did the things they did, and still do.

Here's a couple of snippets from chapters in this volume, **Boots on the Ground** which begins with Jamaca's historical and political background and what brought me to Jamaica and into Kingston's inner cities, following through to 2004.

Hellshire Blessings:

When we reached Miss Icy's (a woman in her eighties and bedridden), I observed Javaughan and Reds laughing, joking and listening to her tell the same story three times in thirty minutes. They changed her bed linen and nightie. They propped her up and warmed up some food and all with an ease that said, "we have done this, many times". I had heard the stories of these two boys and found it hard to reconcile the cold-blooded enforcers that I knew them to be (yes at fourteen and sixteen years of age), with the youngsters in front of me, feeding Miss Icy, wiping the dribble from her chin, engaging with her, enjoying her laughter and helping her on and off her commode.

I recognised the joy these young men gave and received as we went through the day, and in the long reasonings that followed I realised that the "good s'maddy" (good person), is who they wanted to be, but circumstances and situations dictated otherwise.

Javaughan's father died when he was a toddler and he was left behind in the care of an aunt when his mother emigrated without telling him it was going to happen. He was seven years old. The aunt had no interest in him, other than the money that arrived regularly through Western Union, but from which, he benefitted little. The only malice he ever held towards her was for burning the only picture he had of his parents together, (which was also the only one of his father) in order to punish him for not sweeping out the house. Shortly after that incident, his mother was killed in a car crash in Miami, leaving him an orphan at ten years old. His aunt just disappeared. Javaughan came home from school to find her and her things gone, never to be heard from again. In less than six months he had lost the only family he knew.

Javaughan was then taken in by Miss Rose, one of his mother's elderly "church mothers". The arrangement worked well for them and she took good care of him, as he did of her until she too died some twelve months later. Homeless and alone, he dropped out of school and slept wherever he could until he was offered a room and a 'job' by the local Don.

Reds on the other hand, saw his mother almost daily, often passed out on the corner by the gully, crack pipe nearby. She had been an addict for as long as Reds could remember. Her brain was so destroyed she no longer remembered her one child, often begging from him like a stranger, even offering him sex for the price of a rock of crack. He did his best to stay far from her, yet still saw no-one took liberties with her and that a box of cooked food was sent to her morning and evening with a bottle of water, even fresh clothes.

His compassion towards her was impressive, as he said to me more than once,

"Mi know seh dem seh shi wukliss, but Jah know, shi a mi mudda, a shi gimme life, mi affi luv har still, mi fi care har, don't Miss Myra?" (*I know they say she is worthless, but God knows, she is my mother, she gave me life, I have to love her for that, I have to take care of her, isn't that right Miss Myra*)

Teacher

As Camp opened up, children literally two and three years of age turned up, mainly as they were being cared for by older siblings whilst mummy, grandma or even great-grandma, looked about 'back to school' (preparing for new school year). What was I going to do with these babies? We had use of the Church, the Basic School and the Centre, so we moved the babies into one class area of the basic school. There was one corner youth named Damon, who had no family of the ages for Camp and could potentially pose a bit of a problem as his lack of literacy skills made him unpredictable. As far as he saw, everyone was 'getting' something out of the programme except him and he was feeling uncomfortable about it.

Damon was nineteen or twenty years old, eyes as cold as steel, a temper that was quick and could be fatal, definitely not a man to cross. Clad as usual in slippers, mesh merino and cut-off jeans with one leg rolled up, he watched me with the baby-class. I saw him slide in beside Kimo (four years old), who was singing the alphabet. Damon joined in the singing and I saw him smile for the first time in the two years I had known him, a real, genuine smile. I sent the little ones into the playground to await lunch and called Damon over into the office.

"Damon, you know I am really swamped. I can't be in the classroom with the babies and on the road getting food and stuff for the children, you could help me out?"

"Miss Myra, yuh dun know seh mi cyaan read" (*"Miss Myra, you already know that I can't read"*)

"But you don't need to, just sing them their ABC, 123, play two games and kick two balls with them, it would really help me out."

The following morning Damon turned up, on time, in his usual attire. I didn't mention this, just his presence was enough for me and his willingness to do me a favour. At the end of the day he brought us both a cold Red Stripe (local beer) and sat with me in the office, a smile on his face like you rarely see from anyone, it lit up the whole room, sipping on his beer, he looked at me and said,

"Mi know wha mi a go do tomorrow, dem nice, tanks y'hear", got up and left. (*"I know what I'm going to do tomorrow, they are nice, thanks, you hear?"*)

Wednesday, Damon arrived punctually, but this time, dressed in black church pants, polished black church shoes, white merino under a pressed shirt and a smile. I was a little surprised, to say the least, I smiled back.

"Is wha Miss Myra?" (*"What you looking at Miss Myra?"*)

"I'm just loving the look."

"So wha'ppen, yuh nuh seh mi a teacher?" (*"So what's wrong, didn't you say I am a teacher?"*)

"Well, yes"

"So, mi nuh fi look like a one?" (*"So, shouldn't I look like one?"*)

"I am impressed".

At the end of Camp, when he received his Certificate of Appreciation and a framed picture of him and his class, he hugged me up tight.

"Miss Myra, yuh dun know. Seriously tho' yuh see when di pickney dem look pon mi, hands up an a please sir, please sir, is different, dem don't scared, dem love mi an respec mi, Jah know seh is different!!". (*"Miss Myra, you know how it goes. Seriously though, when the children look up at me, hands up, please sir, please sir, it feels different, they're not scared of me, they love me and respect me, God knows it feels different!!"*)

PREFACE

Time to write THE book. Why? There really is somuch to say. This morning, the 7th August 2016 with so many memories flooding my brain, I feel the urge to start writing again, and really focus on "the book". I honestly haven't felt that urge since a fire in 2009 stole fifteen years of my valuable journals and diaries that held my innermost thoughts, prayers and very precious, heart wrenching, loving and fun memories, plus untold photographs.

Today, however, I kinda got the urge, it is time, time to tell the stories while the memories hold. When I got up this morning, it was not the best of days, a very upsy downsy kind of morning, STRESS...... Took a minute to check my Facebook page (that soon became an hour), I checked the stress of others and realised, I don't have any really!

I have the most incredible number of blessings, I have a large, loving, compassionate, passionate, forward thinking, supportive, not afraid to step out of the box and live their dreams, family and circle of friends. I have lived a life full of spice and variety (and I don't mean men).

I have been blessed to have moved amongst some of our greatest Reggae and Soul artistes, worldwide, in studios, at home and socially. I have laughed and reasoned with great singers, players of instruments and philosophers, although I can't tell an A note from a B note, I know what "sounds" right.

I have fought alongside some of the greatest activists for community change, from Erin Pizzey during the birth of the first UK refuge for battered women with Chiswick Women's Aid, across all areas of need and oppression to JFJ (Jamaicans for Justice) and Jamaican children in need, for well over 45 years.

I have sat down, reasoned, laughed and cried with youth in gangs, gang leaders and don men (and women), in the prisons and on the streets, and with families of, and victims of crime. I have watched Jamaica change, not always (rarely actually) for the better, but I love Jamaica same way.

I see so many of the youth I have known throughout their growing up years, making the most incredible strides in their lives. Little girls I watched singing into their hair brushes, posing in the mirror, becoming singers at all levels, from local school music teacher to big international artistes. Little boys, who would drive everyone crazy bang-banging on every surface becoming artistes, producers, players of instruments, again at all levels. Young boys and girls, who have become the most amazing adults, some raising even more incredible boys and girls who will exceed all expectations and yes, I will big up my chest, proud that I know them personally. I have no shame about claiming my "Aunty" status amongst them (smile).

Then there is the whole pack of youth who have found their niche in life and are now raising fabulous families filled with love and who change lives daily by how they live and what they do.

Do you realise how blessed that makes me? Well honestly, until this morning, I didn't...... and I have barely scratched the surface.

God has His own plans and His plans have taken me through adventures, joys, sorrows, pain and laughter, bringing me safely through.

In writing this book, I have changed some names, not just to protect others, the characters and events are real. For some, the only record of their existence is in these pages. Some were born, lived and died without any kind of registration, young, old and in between, known only as reference numbers.

JAMAICA TIMELINE

1494 - Christopher Columbus arrived in Jamaica, then inhabited by the Taino or Arawak nation, whose population was decimated through disease and enslavement. Jamaica is colonized by the Spanish.

1655 - Jamaica is colonized by the British

1692 - Port Royal destroyed by earthquake

1834 - Slave trade abolished

1838 - Emancipation of slaves

1907 - Kingston destroyed by earthquake

1938 - Labour unrest leads to the formation of the first political party, the People's National Party (PNP) and the first trade union, the Bustamante Industrial Trade Union (BITU), out of which the Jamaica Labour Party (JLP) was formed.

1944 - Universal adult suffrage – everyone gets a vote.
1962 - Independence from Britain – though remains part of Commonwealth.

Prime Ministers

1962 - 1967 - Sir Alexander Bustamante   JLP

1967 – 1967 – Sir Donald Sangster (Feb-Apr)
        (died of a brain haemorrhage)   JLP

1967 – 1972 – Hon. Hugh L Shearer   JLP

1972 – 1980 – Hon. Michael Manley   PNP

1980 – 1989 – Right Hon. Edward Seaga   JLP

1989 – 1992 – Hon. Michael Manley   PNP

1992 – 2006 – Most Right Hon. Percival
        J Patterson   PNP

2006 – 2007 – Most Hon. Portia Simpson-Miller PNP

2007 – 2011 – Most Hon. Bruce Golding   JLP

2011 – 2012 – Most Hon. Andrew Holness   JLP

2012 – 2016 – Most Hon. Portia Simpson-Miller PNP

2016 –   - Most Hon. Andrew Holness   JLP

Politics

The lead up to the 1980 general election was the bloodiest yet with an official figure of over seven hundred dead in that year alone! I have often heard it referred to as the 'Political War' and though not officially recognised as such, the fall out and long-term consequences have been (and continue to be), the same.
The Maulers and The Pigeon Gang were names I remember

caused fear as they fought to maintain control of streets and parts of streets. Turf borders were literally down or across the middle of streets, across empty lots and corner to corner. The political violence divided and devastated communities, streets and even families. Jamaica has never been the same since. Local feuds were created which resulted in a refusal by the Dons (political and community gang leaders) to return the arms to the politicians. The Dons utilising the same routes and links they had used to bring in the guns and export ganja (Marijuana) to pay for them on behalf of the politicians, began doing so for themselves. Large numbers who had done favours for the politicians, together with others fleeing the violence, migrated legally and illegally to the U.S.A., Canada and the U.K.

The political 'war' totally decimated the communities and community spirit in every way possible. With many original residents being run out in order to move in the correct 'vote', they were made to choose between political allegiance and family loyalties, life-long friends and neighbours. Thus the 'Garrison' was born and has yet to be dismantled. Zinc fences were erected to a) deter gunmen from running through the yard b) provide a series of concealed pathways from one street to the next, for gunmen and c) conceal persons and activities going on in yards. They have remained in place ever since and still provide the same coverage, some by different routes. The Garrisons are usually in high population, low employment, urban, poor communities, overseen by one or more 'Dons' who maintain control of the community's legal and illegal activities, here and abroad. The 'Dons' are supported in their endeavours by a series of 'corner-men' who are usually responsible for maintaining discipline and look out for his road and also by 'foot-soldiers' who are at the bidding of them both. It's a wee bit like the army; you have the General, the Sergeant Major and the Squaddie, which I suppose in reality they are, in their community.

The scarce resources of the country were (and still are) controlled by whichever political party was in power at the time, supposedly to the benefit of their voters, but actually being used to control constituents to the benefit of the fund holders.

The well documented US government fears and paranoia concerning Communism, Castro and Cuba, prompted CIA interference in the political process through the importation of guns to arm and ensure victory for the more favourable, conservative party of the two. Ganja (Marijuana) and later Cocaine, became the currency to pay for arms on both sides of the political divide, providing the seed ground for the "Yardie" gangs that have since taken hold in the U.K., U.S.A. and Canada. The 'war' created divisions, enmities and feuds between communities, sections of communities, friends, neighbours and even within families, which continue to this day.

Much of this animosity and feuding migrates with them when they get the chance to go to 'foreign'. Since that time the corner and community dons have emerged, fighting one another in reprisal for past or current sins, control of local political or community turf, control of drugs turf here and abroad and of course, the scamming for which Jamaica has become so infamous. Since that time, each generation has become more violent. Educational and employment opportunities are less readily available, particularly if you have certain addresses.

There is not a child since 1979/1980 that has grown up in the inner cities, without knowledge or experience of the repercussions of the 1980 election, regular gunshots, death of family and friends, lawlessness, jungle justice and feudal control by the local Dons. Levels of violence have increased more and more intensely because each man must make his own mark. As a consequence of this, what was once abhorrent, impossible, a no-no, totally unacceptable, has now become acceptable and even the norm.

ACKNOWLEDGEMENTS

A huge shout out and thanks:

To my incredible children, Tammie, Angie, Josie and Lee. To my fabulous grandchildren, Paige, Dierre, Damar, Marley, Olivia, Tye, Jada, Maliaka, Faith and Evy. To all who have supported my every step, even when not necessarily agreeing with the steps I've taken.

To my amazing siblings who have cared for, supported and nurtured my children and grandchildren in my many long absences, encouraging and enabling them to be the incredible young people they are.

To my Miracle Church family in Bedford whose members and Women's Happy Hour group continue to support us over the years with Prayer and financial aid.

To Chris and Andy, without your help so many children would not have had a chance, some made good, some not so good but you have made and continue to make the most amazing difference to so many.

To the singers and players, teachers, priests, pastors, and media personnel who have supported in all kinds of ways.

To all the residents of Kingston, especially Kingston 11, who have welcomed me for so long and made the journey possible. Thank you again. Without your support and patience, this book would not be possible

To Aunty Chris Maher, thanks for your support, guidance and heavy use of the editor's red pen, bringing me to the final drafts.

To Tony Kelly, thank you for your editing of the final drafts, checking my patois translations and history.

HOW IT ALL BEGAN

FOUNDATION

P eople have asked me if I am ever scared. "Yes" is the answer to that question, many, times over, but there is a spirit inside that finds it hard to give in to the fear, perhaps it's the rebel Weafer/Griffin genes!!.

I was born the fourth of eight children in Dublin, into a large, strong, Irish, Catholic family, often not the most functional, but always the most giving, passionate and compassionate people. We moved to London in the late 1950's, starting in one room until eventually buying a large old house in Highbury, north London in the 1960's.

Service to others was a daily reality practised by all we knew. From the sharing of breakfast with others attending early Mass (because my daddy knew that they were going home to nothing) to making space for a variety of life's waifs and strays in need of a safe temporary space. This was not because we were well off, God knows we weren't, but as Mum and Daddy would say, "there is always someone worse off and no matter how little there is, there is always enough to share". I cannot say I was always appreciative of the sentiment, especially when watching my favourite big Sunday breakfast, designed to feed ten, being stretched to feed fifteen or more.

Daddy was involved with Crisis at Christmas and other programmes caring for the homeless. While Mum immersed herself in the Unions, the Women's Movement and the Optimist

Swimming Club (for people with disabilities), which she served for close to fifty years.   Both worked full time and had second jobs for many, many years.

We were taught to watch out for each other and our elderly neighbours, often carrying them a bowl of Daddy's Wednesday soup or stew to warm up a winter's evening.

We had maternal grandparents nearby who were always available and had the best Sunday Tea table in the world, with trifle and sandwiches, cakes and scones, which were a real treat. They were also rebels and pioneers in the Irish Adoption Society, resulting in the legal formalisation of adoption in Ireland through the Adoption Act 1952. Our paternal grandparents and family residing in Ireland were more distant. They were teachers and caregivers who served internationally through religious missionary orders.   We were always surrounded by books and music of all kinds. Knowledge was always available and wisdom close at hand.

It is no surprise that even to this day, that same gene-pool is producing passionate and compassionate pioneers, innovators, care givers, entrepreneurs, artists, musicians and happy, functional families who care about and for each other and their wider communities.

We grew in a racially mixed area of London at a time when racism was overt and adverts for rented accommodation, in windows and on shop notice boards read, "No children, No blacks, No dogs, No Irish"!!! The Irish and the Caribbean communities, feeling the same oppression, with the same love of music, dance and the spoken word and fear of God (Church), were drawn together and often lived and socialized as we did, in close proximity. Inevitably, some of us would become romantically involved and have bi-racial families.

Over the years, I moved within the music and performing arts circles using my administration skills to assist a number of Jamaican musicians and artistes with setting up their own publishing and performing rights portfolios to help ensure they received the monies due from their recordings and performances.

I first travelled to Jamaica in 1977, with my then husband Barry, who came from Clarendon and had spent much of his pre-teen years in Tower Hill, Kingston 11 with his aunt and uncle. He joined them in London in 1964. We met and married in 1973 and came to visit the family with two small daughters aged five and three, in 1977, just before the 'war' for the 1980 election began. We divided our three months stay between the family in Clarendon and those in Kingston. At that time, Hagley Park and Waltham Park were still 'toppa narris', that is, middle class and upper middle-class communities, with large family houses on good sized, well-fruited plots. Tower Hill, Cockburn Pen, Bay Farm Villa, Compound, Marl Road, Cling-Cling, White Wing, Belrock, although having their own separate community names, were all one community until the 'war'.

Between my stay in 1977 and the general election of 1980, Kingston 11, politically divided as it was, became a hotbed of violence with supporters on either side going on regular looting and shooting sprees. I heard tales during that time of vile, cruel and wicked deeds on both sides of the political divide and not just in Kingston 11.

Being married to a Jamaican from the area, during the late 1970's and early 1980's in London, I got to know a lot of the 'soldiers' and survivors from both sides and when I reflect on it, a significant number from Kingston 11. During those same years, I watched the impact this had on Jamaican society in the UK, the way it changed the face of the "shebeens" gambling houses and street vibes. Reggae artistes came regularly to North and North-West London and South London. The Friday and Saturday night "parties" became divided on Jamaican political lines and where the arguments used to be over girl and money, it was now often littered with political slurs, calls of "dutty Labourite" (JLP) this and "stinking PNP" that. This changed with the rise of the Dub systems playing at local Universities and colleges, bringing a diverse following across the racial and socioeconomic spectrum. Dancehall had its own separate following playing in the smaller clubs and venues, often controlled by the local 'Yardie" bosses. It has always amused me that the JLP or Jamaica Labour Party, unlike the UK Labour party, is the more conservative, right leaning political party and the PNP or People's National Party the more socialist, left leaning party.

I have lived in and moved around freely in the inner cities of Kingston, assisting with community development and education since 2001. I have seen the reckless firing of arms by both the authorities and the communities, unconcerned that women and children were in the line of fire.

I have listened to the stories of the atrocities carried out both during and since the political 'war' in Jamaica, from both victims and perpetrators.

I have witnessed the results of some of the punishments administered for or by the corner men and Dons, as no one has any faith in the justice system.

I have watched young people rise above it all and become the success that is featured on talk shows, others who manage to keep their head above the goings on and struggle to maintain their families and keep them safe, on a daily basis.

I have met some so traumatised by what they have seen, heard, experienced or done, that they can no longer feel pain, love or happiness, they are empty.

I have watched the light of hope die in a child's eye and come to the realisation that the purpose in the life of some is to take the lives of others. And yet, I have never met one killer who does not regret the taking of that first life, in the words of more than one:

"From you take a life, you have to start disregard the value of human life because otherwise, you can't live with what you did.

Then after a while, you find it doesn't affect you anymore and is easier to take another". A truly soul-destroying statement, one which haunts me daily.

Here in Jamaica, there is a saying that they 'tek serious ting an mek joke' (*find the funny side of any situation*), so I have tried to retain the humour and see the funny side. Not always possible, but I have tried.

For those readers unfamiliar with Jamaican Patois, translations are bracketed and initalics.

1977 - 1998

So, let's start at the beginning:

When I came to Jamaica in 1977, we spent about six weeks staying with Ms Dada at 48 Tamarind Turn, Kingston 11, off Tower Avenue. Ms Dada was the mother of my aunt-in-law, Lynette Dyke. The zinc fences weren't there in those days, just a nice vibe, with some lanes like 'country', in 'town'.

In 1995, whilst working in the reggae music industry in the UK, I returned to spend eight weeks in Jamaica meeting with musicians, artistes and producers. During my visit I stayed with family friends in Patrick City, we only drove through Kingston 11 from place to place, not walking, just not recognizing the place at all.

The Tower Hill and Cockburn Pen I had encountered on my first visit in 1977 had changed beyond all recognition. No-one could possibly recognise the community I spent time in during 1995 as being the same place I had first visited. In 1977, Kingston 11 appeared an up and coming, working class, residential community, bordering the busy factory lined Spanish Town Road and the middle-class communities of Waltham Park and Hagley Park. I remember the chicken wire fences separating the yards, with picket gates painted the same colour as the house. Some of the houses were board, some concrete and steel and even some wattle and daub. I don't remember seeing grills on windows, yes on some concrete house verandas, the newer ones, but not windows.

The intervening years, with the 'war' over the 1980 election had transformed and separated the communities, not just physically, but the whole vibe of Kingston 11 had changed totally. It had become a series of zinc fenced garrison enclaves, whose residents were socially and economically, impoverished and disenfranchised by events and traumatised by what they experienced and witnessed.

When I next came back to Jamaica, in February 1998, it was to rest, have a break, enjoy the sunshine and spend time with people who had become good friends and say goodbye to others who had passed. My life course was changed, I would never again be the same. The Jamaica which had taken my heart in 1977, now took my spirit, my very being.

In 1998, gunshot was the nightly lullaby for most residents. Fear was tangible, no-one trusted anyone anymore, with some communities ruled by a single Don (local community/political gang leader), others with a different Don on every corner. Police and troops drove through the streets regularly and good citizens stayed home after dark even if there was no curfew. I remember Miss Tunny calling Lukie and Danny to check where they were and advise of any unsavoury action in or near, letting them know whether or not it was safe to drive in.

Miss Tunny was the mother of Danny Bassie one of the Jamaican musicians I had met and assisted over the years in London. She was a slight, yet sturdy, dark skinned, grey haired woman in her mid-seventies. Her room was to the back of the concrete block and steel house near her favourite spot, the original house constructed of wood and now the kitchen. She, Danny and her two daughters Prim (plus her two sons) and Dulcie (plus her two sons) lived together in the family yard. Lukie (Dulcie's elder son) had built his own couple of rooms onto the side of the house for him and his family. Lukie is a renowned reggae singer, Danny a musician, a producer and member of The Fire House Crew, the reggae and dancehall band. He is proficient in several instruments and acclaimed for his mastery of the five stringed bass-guitar.

The family made me welcome and their dynamics a reminder of my own dysfunctional, caring, compassionate family.

That first trip of 1998 saw me spend most of my time at Delisser Avenue, in the kitchen and yard with Miss Tunny, Dulcie and Prim, making trips to the various music recording studios with Lukie or the Fire House Crew, cultural reggae icon Luciano and master musician, saxophone impresario, musical director and producer Dean Fraser. I alternated studio days with lazy days on Hellshire Beach. During that time, I was drawn more and more to returning, my plan to do more of the same.

CRICKET

Following my visit in February 1998, during which time I had met a group of youngsters who grabbed my heart, I returned in November to spend my first Christmas in the sun. My family had clubbed together for my "Christmas Box" and with that added to my savings, I knew I had enough to see the children around me had a nice time and they would have something to 'work' with after the holiday.

Danny picked me up from the Norman Manley Airport, Kingston and as we drove into Delisser Avenue, I could see the welcome committee gathered outside number 13. They were excitedly waving at the car as we approached, some of them running towards us. I cannot lie, I felt like a film star or royalty as I got out of the car to hugs and kisses and "Welcome home" cheers from all directions, children and adults alike, certainly not what I had expected!

Miss Tunny greeted me with a plate of rice and peas, plantain and a huge fried Parrot fish alongside a glass of chilled coconut water, a smile as wide as the Nile and a hug that could heal any hurt. It was a good hour of hugs before I could sit back, eat and follow the meal with a large, iced, rum cream. Yes, I was HOME.

Next morning, Dulcie ever up before the dawn, could be heard rattling around in the kitchen out back making "coffee-tea". In Jamaica every hot beverage has the additional tag of tea, so you have Milo-tea, Chocolate-tea etc. The tantalising aroma drifted across the yard, through the house to Dulcie's room which I was staying in, at the front of the house. She was Studio One artiste and back-up singer on many tunes produced by the Godfather of Reggae, Clement "Coxson" Dodd (who taught me to how to mix music 'Studio 1' stylee). Dulcie and I had become good friends when she and her younger son were in London in the late Spring of 1997. A well-built woman with a very large behind that had earned her the pet name 'Dulcimina' (an old-fashioned large travel bag), or 'Dulcie' for short.

By the time I bathed and came back to Dulcie's room, breakfast, and I do mean BREAKFAST, was on the table. A veritable feast of the Jamaican National Dish ackee and saltfish with crisply fried dumplings (which were light, just melt in the mouth), coffee-tea (sweet and strong) and freshly squeezed orange juice. We dined, laughed 'til we cried, caught up on gossip, sobbed and hugged as we mourned and consoled one another at the death of so many in my short absence.

By seven a.m. I heard Ms. Tunny trying to run the children from the gate. They just took a step back, laughed and moved forward again so I went out and Ms. Tunny let them into the yard. We sat under the large old Guinep tree and, horrified when I perched on a concrete building block, Dulcie came rushing out with one of her dining chairs. Guinep is a favourite during the Autumn months, a small round fruit in a thick, green skin that when popped open between the teeth, looks and tastes a bit like Lychee.

I listened as the children chatted, catching up on who was doing well at school and who was not doing so well. With big dramatic gestures and much interrupting of one another, they filled me in on what was happening in the community, who was dead and who killed them, who went to 'foreign' *(overseas)*, who went to prison, who chop who, for what and who was 'bunning' who, with who *(being unfaithful)*. Never believe children don't know what is going on, their eyes and ears are sharp!

I heard the grumble of some bellies so I asked who would like to 'run a boat' (*an impromptu, spur of the moment cook up*) for me because I was hungry. Dulcie gave me a stern look from the veranda but brought out two coal stoves anyway. Javaughan and Reds, always the leaders, headed off to Ms. Mitzy at the corner shop and bought 5lbs of rice, four tins of mackerel, two packs of disposable plates, disposable forks and a bag of coal. Sixty minutes later, breakfast all round and everybody was happy. Already bursting at the seams from Dulcie's feast, it was hard to find room for the plateful placed before me by Javaughan. However, having declared I was hungry, it would make the children feel I was scorning their efforts or worse, pitied them, if I did not partake. I made a brave effort and was so relieved when another youngster arrived so I had an excuse to share the rest of the food on my plate.

Javaughan was slim, dark skinned and threatening to be tall. A handsome boy with a winning smile and mischief ever present in his eyes, he was a kindly spirit with a dry sense of humour. He could tell a tale, play every character in it, full of drama and jokes, making everyone else fall apart with laughter, all without changing the deadpan expression on his face, though the sparkle in his eye could not be missed. He was what you would call, a loveable rogue. At barely fourteen, he was already a seasoned 'foot soldier' and enforcer for his local 'Don'.

I'm not quite sure how Reds earned his pet name, because his skin was black like Ebony and shone with a bluish hue. So, it was somewhat of a surprise to hear him referred to as Reds, a name normally reserved for those with light coloured skin. A more serious looking young man, Reds was determined he would leave the community one day.

You could always rely on a good laugh when the two of them were together. Their re-enactments of the community dramas from the night before, between neighbours, girls on the road and the men in the bars, were the highlight of my day.

I asked the children what it was that they all liked doing

best and of course, sports was the number one answer and reality is they had little access to or knowledge of any other pursuits. The decision was made to go and buy some balls and other sports equipment, so off I went to take public transport. Ms. Tunny almost fainted at the prospect and with her dire warnings ringing in my ears, escorted by Javaughan and Reds we headed to Giscombe's, the big sporting goods store in Half Way Tree. Half Way Tree is the main shopping district sitting half way between Uptown (New Kingston) and Downtown (Central Kingston). I spoke to the manager, explaining that I wanted to set the children up with a little sports club. After a call to the proprietor, a massive discount enabled us to buy half a dozen footballs, basketballs and netballs, two senior cricket sets and one junior set.

The available land-space required clearing, levelling and rolling to make a safe playing area, so next up was a trip across to Waterhouse to borrow a roller from a contractor friend named Mr. Binns and to arrange delivery. He kindly agreed to this but unfortunately, he couldn't drop it off until after four p.m. the next day.

Next morning, I woke up to the clang-clang-clang-clang of stone on gate and twenty plus children outside, it was six a.m.!

"Miss Myra, Miss Myra, yuh nah come play cricket??" (*Miss Myra, Miss Myra aren't you coming to play cricket??*")

"But we have no roller until this afternoon. We haven't even cleared the land yet"

"Oh yes Miss Myra, wi ready"

As I looked across the bottom of the Avenue onto Raniford (the waste land between Diamond Road and Simon Taylor Road, bordering Tower Hill, Cockburn Pen and Waterhouse), there in front of my eyes was a beautifully cleared, flat and compacted area with Mr. Binns' roller lying down at the top end.

My first thought was "How did they get it here?" my second thought, fully cognisant of the enmity between the two communities, was a more nervous, "Is what o'clock did they go over there?"

I quickly called over to check with Mr. Binns that he was aware we had his roller.

"Is wha yuh do wid dem y'ere pickney? dem bright yuh know. A t'ree o'clock bells dem cum knock mi gates. Lucky seh mi nuh reach mi bed yet, tell mi seh dem a go push it across. Mi laugh til mi weak" (*What do you do with those youngsters? They're cheeky, three o'clock they came knocking, luckily, I wasn't in bed yet, told me they were going to push it across. I laughed until I was weak*)

"So, you really drove over here at those hours?"

"Yuh mussi mad, dem nuh seh dem a guh push it?" (*"You must be mad, didn't they say they were going to push it?"*)

And so, they did, six determined young men passed through Binns Road Waterhouse, along "Wailers" and out to Spanish Town Road to Diamond Road and round to Simon Taylor, across various unfriendly 'turfs', and that is far, never mind pushing a half-ton roller.

Watching them setting up the wicket and marking the boundaries, so full of joy and anticipation, it came to me just how much these lads had risked for a simple game of cricket.

I asked Javaughan a couple of years later how they did it. At three a.m. any turf is on watch and ready to shoot at anything that moves.

"Wen we lef yuh di night, mi guh check two a di links dem, mek dem know seh wi a cum look fi Mr. Binns when 'im back from di bar, cos wi did kno seh 'im a go a roun robin. So, di links mek dem soldiers know seh wi cum tru', seh a fi di white lady ova Lukie yard. Yuh name gud long time. The Dread tell hevrybaddy 'bout how yuh deal wid 'im an 'im fambily. Yuh name big yuh dun know!" (*"When we left you that night, we went to see some people I know, told them we were coming to look for Mr. Binns, but late, because we knew he was going to be at the local bar. They let those on watch know that we were coming across, saying it was for the white lady staying over by Lukie. Your name is respected from time. The Dread told everyone how you looked after him and his family. You're famous don't you know!")*

HELLSHIRE BLESSINGS

Happy to be back in Jamaica at Delisser Avenue in November 1998, away from the wintry weather back home, as usual, the children from the block gravitated towards me and we would sit on the veranda and rap. A few of them were eager to show me how well they had done in school since we last met. We decided that a trip to the beach was in order to celebrate everyone's efforts. I set about finding the necessary transport to carry us to Hellshire beach, some forty minutes away in the neighbouring parish of St Catherine. We had arranged with a local shopkeeper to borrow his minibus to take us there and back, however, on the day we had double the children anticipated. I made some calls but unfortunately, no one had a bus available because there were a couple of big funerals in the locality. I called on Dean Fraser, told him my predicament and he immediately offered his truck, however there was a slight drawback, he could only do the outward trip as he was performing later in the day.

We gathered together in the Trinitarian Church on Delisser, three adults and thirty-eight children, aged from three to sixteen years. All the children were dressed to the nines in their "going-out-in" clothes with their towels and swimsuits at the ready. I was seated beside a young girl named Lacey and her little sister, Nanny, who became a shadow that for a few years, followed me everywhere.

"Mith Myra, you can sthwim?" *("Miss Myra, can you swim?")*

"Yes sweetie, since I was little"

"Fi real? ow come mi hear thay, white people nuh like wata?" *{"Really? How come I heard white people don't like water?")*

In pipes Lacey, "Is tru' dem nuh like bathe" *("Because they don't like to bathe")*

With a deep inhale of breath, Nanny smells my neck and responds, "Hey but Miss Myra bathe, sthe sthmell thweet yuh kno, cum ssthmell har nuh!!!" *("Hey, but Miss Myra bathes, she smells sweet you know, come and smell her then!!!")*

I was still laughing when Dean Fraser's truck arrived and eighteen children jammed into the back heading off to Hellshire, followed by the rest of us, all crammed into a twelve-seater minibus.

The children totally relaxed, played together joyfully without arguing!! I was flabbergasted to see such a difference in the children who at home would trace *(call one another names)* and cuss one another on sight, daily, for no reason.

By two p.m. everyone was famished. I approached a vendor who had been supplying us with drinks at discounted prices, uncertain as to how far my seven thousand Jamaican dollars would go towards feeding forty-one of us. I gave her the numbers, she laughed with a bellow that belied her tiny frame, hands on hips she asked, "is a miracle yuh look?" *("you're looking for a miracle?")* Straight faced I said "yes", which made her laugh some more. Without hesitation, she picked up a bucket and proceeded to approach the other vendors around her hut, informing them of our dilemma. With much finger pointing, nodding of heads and riotous laughter, between them all we were served with enough fish, bammy *(a traditional Jamaican cassava flatbread)*, festival *(Caribbean fried sweet dumpling)* and bag juice to fill everyone's belly, and all within our budget of seven thousand Jamaican dollars.

As I relaxed I was approached by a gentleman of middle years,

"Excuse me Miss Myra is it I hear di dem pickney say? I'm Winston, I see yuh is here with a heap a pickney, is which school?" *("Excuse me, Miss Myra, is it that I hear the children call you? I'm Winston, I see you are here with a heap of children, from which school")*

"Various schools, these live around where I am staying in Cockburn Pen" (pronounced Cock-Burn).

"Cockburn Pen? Kingston 11, Cockburn Pen?!"

"Yes, same one."

"But you're white, where you from?"

"Irish by birth, spent most of my life in London though."

"Is really Pen pickney a behave so nice?" *("Are they really children from Cockburn Pen and behaving so well?")*

"Yep" I replied with a chest bursting with pride and a grin from ear to ear.

With that he handed me four thousand Jamaican dollars and said: "Well lady, mi wan yuh fi tek dis and treat di pickney dem, dem nice, mi proud a dem." *("Well lady, I want you to take this and give the children a treat, they're nicely behaved, I'm proud of them.")*

We were thrilled to bits, now a decision had to be made by the children as to how it would be spent.

Later that evening as we sat in the yard, we talked it through and deduced that as we had already purchased cricket equipment, footballs, netballs, basketballs and had hoops, sports equipment was not a necessity, so what else was essential? The kids decided, NOTHING!! Javaughan asked,

"Wi can do someting fi di elder dem?, wi dun get treat a'ready, wi ave nuff tings, wi nuh need nutten". *("Can we do something for the elderly? We've had treats already, we have enough things, we don't need anything.")*

Armed with their four thousand Jamaican dollars and my Christmas money from home, two of the boys and two of the girls accompanied me to the wholesalers at Three Miles to see how far we could stretch our cash and what we could acquire with it. Our target was to give fifty elders a little blessing for the holiday, this we conveyed to the owners who helped with huge discounts and 'brawta' *(free extras)*. A friendly taxi-driver assisted us by collecting all our purchases and delivering them to Delisser Avenue free of charge. How awesome was that?!

The excitement of the children was explosive when they saw the goods arrive, they flocked into the yard, ready and eager to help bag-up and distribute their gifts. Javaughan commandeered a set of scales from Miss Mitzy's in front of Trinitarian. He also obtained some wood and old wheels (actually, two of them were not so old), and with the combined efforts of two others and much (mumbled) cursing, they created a strong cart on which to deliver the gifts to the elders in the neighbourhood.

As we weighed and bagged two hundred pounds of rice, one hundred pounds of sugar, two hundred pounds of flour, all in two-pound bags it became easier and easier to fill the bags with the correct amount so that as it touched the scales, it was bang on.

Ricky, a lovely eight year old boy, bright, painfully slim, (with the most expressive eyes I have ever looked into) and as we would say, 'very mannersable' *(polite)*, watched carefully as bag after bag weighed exactly two pounds on the scale.

"Miss Myra, is how yuh do dat?" *(Miss Myra, how do you do that?")*

"What sweetie?"

"Yuh nuh si seh ebry time is a proppa, proppa two poun yuh put inna di bag?" *("Don't you see that every time, it's exactly 2lb you put in the bag?")*

"That's cos I'm magic"

"Fi real?!!" *("Really?!!")*

"Yep, bet I can tell you which subject you don't like"

"Untruth!!! tell mi den nuh" *("Don't believe you, tell me then")*

"Maths"

Jumping off the stool, knocking over piles of tinned Bully beef, mackerel and sardines, eyes almost out of his head, he cried out,

"Is 'ow yuh know dat?" *("How do you know that?")*

"I never tell you say, I was magic?" *("Didn't I tell you I had magical power?)*

I never told him that I had yet to meet an eight-year-old in Jamaica that actually did like maths, so it was a pretty safe bet. From that moment on, I had a reputation amongst the children for magic or 'science'.

It took us all day to bag up fifty packages of basic food and another fifty of toiletries. The following day I was to make the most life-changing trip of my life, on foot through the lanes from Belrock at Three Miles down to Delisser Avenue.

Escorted by thirty plus children, aged six to sixteen years, we started our mission. Commencing at Belrock we visited four lone elders and presented them with our gifts. Moving through the roads and lanes between Spanish Town Road and Olympic Way we made our way down towards Delisser Avenue. The condition of some of the elders we visited (all of whom were known either to Javaughan or Reds), was such that to this day the sights, smells and living conditions still haunt my sleep.

Reds was sixteen years old at that time, a survivor. He had a very, NOT NICE side to him, in fact, a distinctly dangerous one, but when he was with the elders, he had this incredibly gentle, caring, compassionate side that just exploded from him. His face and eyes would glow with a light that otherwise remained hidden. Javaughan too lit up with a brightness I only ever saw when we were with the elders, as though these were their safe spaces, where they were accepted for who they were and loved by the elders we met. I witnessed the faces of these golden-agers radiate with joy when they saw or heard Javaughan and Reds coming through their gates. That journey showed me just how incredible these two young men were. They had obviously taken the time and effort to know all these elderly individuals, especially the lone elders, and to look out for them.

I knew from experience, from what I had perceived of their movements and their ability to address their own needs and those of the elders' (not to mention the gossip), that these two were not always on the right side of the law. I also knew, from their actions, that they really wanted to see other youth around them stay in school and progress "outta dis place" *("out of the inner city")*. They had a real concern for the elders around them, they were not afraid to deal with the physical needs required by each and every one of these elderly individuals and they did so adeptly.

When we reached Miss Icy's (a woman in her eighties and bedridden), I observed Javaughan and Reds laughing, joking and listening to her tell the same story three times in thirty minutes. They changed her bed linen and nightie. They propped her up and warmed up some food and all with an ease that said, "we have done this, many times". I had heard the stories of these two boys and found it hard to reconcile the cold-blooded enforcers that I knew them to be (yes at fourteen and sixteen years of age), with the youngsters in front of me, feeding Miss Icy, wiping the dribble from her chin, engaging with her, enjoying her laughter and helping her on and off her commode.

I recognised the joy these young men gave and received as we went through the day, and in the long reasonings that followed I realised that the "good s'maddy" *(good person)*, is who they wanted to be, but circumstances and situations dictated otherwise.

Javaughan's father died when he was a toddler and he was

left behind in the care of an aunt when his mother emigrated without telling him it was going to happen. He was seven years old. The aunt had no interest in him, other than the money that arrived regularly through Western Union, but from which, he benefitted little. The only malice he ever held towards her was for burning the only picture he had of his parents together, (which was also the only one of his father) in order to punish him for not sweeping out the house. Shortly after that incident, his mother was killed in a car crash in Miami, leaving him an orphan at ten years old. His aunt just disappeared. Javaughan came home from school to find her and her things gone, never to be heard from again. In less than six months he had lost the only family he knew. Javaughan was then taken in by Miss Rose, one of his mother's elderly "church mothers". The arrangement worked well for them and she took good care of him, as he did of her until she too died some twelve months later. Homeless and alone, he dropped out of school and slept wherever he could until he was offered a room and a 'job' by the local Don.

Reds on the other hand, saw his mother almost daily, often passed out on the corner by the gully, crack pipe nearby. She had been an addict for as long as Reds could remember. Her brain was so destroyed she no longer remembered her one child, often begging from him like a stranger, even offering him sex for the price of a rock of crack. He did his best to stay far from her, yet still saw no-one took liberties with her and that a box of cooked food was sent to her morning and evening with a bottle of water, even fresh clothes. His compassion towards her was impressive, as he said to me more than once,

"Mi know seh dem seh shi wukliss, but Jah know, shi a mi mudda, a shi gimme life, mi affi luv har still, mi fi care har, don't Miss Myra?" ("I know they say she is worthless, but God knows, she is my mother, she gave me life, I have to love her for that, I have to take care of her, isn't that right Miss Myra")

Without family support, they were as so many others, living at the behest of the local Don, 'foot soldiers', one of their jobs, to secure contraband (guns/drugs). Javaughan and Reds chose to use love, care and compassion towards those elders whose yards, outhouses and trees they utilised in their obligations to their 'Don', a very different attitude to that of most of their predecessors, but one maintained by most of those who took over after they were killed.

As I travelled back to London some weeks later, I knew in my heart with all certainty, that:

- gone forever was the retirement plan of winters on a North Coast Beach, sipping rum and Coke from a coconut shell under a palm tree;
- with some help, encouragement and resources the community could do much for itself;
- my knowledge, skills, networks and experience gained in my social, voluntary and professional life, could be passed on to empower and enable others;
- as scary as the increasing violence was in Jamaica at that time (and still is), it felt like home.
- my own children could never know the half of what went on around me in Jamaica!
- my mother could know even less!

1999 TO 2001
SHORT TRIPS

When I returned to the U.K. in January 1999 I thought long and hard about how I could help the elders I had encountered during my recent trip to Jamaica. The living conditions of so many were unimaginable, they had to be seen to be believed. Board houses ready to drop, you dared not step in too heavily as they juddered almost to the point of collapse. Roofs leaking and even whole sheets of zinc missing. Too many elders were immobile, bedridden, uncared for, neglected to the point of abuse, not something I had ever expected to see in Jamaica given my experiences of the Jamaican community in the U.K. These images haunted my sleep. What a difference a little tender loving care would make to their daily lives. Simply, someone to check on them regularly and help them out as needed. I had seen that perfectly demonstrated by Javaughan and Reds during my last visit. They needed a home care service of some sort.

In September 1999 I arrived back in Jamaica for a few weeks to join in the celebrations for Lukie's birthday bashment (party) that was held annually at number 13 Delisser Avenue. Danny came to meet me at the airport and as we approached the gate, I spotted a whole gang of children waiting impatiently. This remarkably warm welcome once more made me feel like a film star, although as I exited the car among the chanting of "Welcome home", there were some complaints of "yuh stay away too long".

Miss Tunny and I retreated to the warm familiar kitchen so she and Dulcie could catch me up on all the happenings in my absence. While warming the fish tea *(a light fish soup)* and frying a huge Parrot fish they imparted heart-rending news of the deaths of several young men and I was heartbroken to hear about one pregnant seventeen-year-old girl, who got caught in the cross-fire.

With approximately fifty or so children and youngsters milling about the yard and hovering around the gate, admittedly it took a little while to convince those in charge that there was nothing untoward happening. The children were quite simply welcoming me home. In those turbulent times, police and troops systematically patrolled the area.

There was a 'camp' at the old paint factory on Diamond Road, therefore, it came as no surprise to see the military at the gate, loudly wanting to know what all the excitement was about. The level of aggression I witnessed, especially towards older boys was sickening. Several youths were hit or 'kuffed' *(punched)* in their necks or the back of their heads for not answering quickly or loudly enough.

Coming as I do from strong, rebel Irish stock, I was not going to stand quietly by and observe such atrocities, certain things are NOT in my nature. I addressed the lead JDF (Jamaica Defence Force) officer in a calm British-Nanny-type tone:

"Sir, can I have a word please?"

"Lady, mi nuh time fi dis, mi wan di yute dem off di street, NOW!!" *("Lady, I don't have time to discuss this, I want the youth off the street NOW!!")*

Observing the increasing crowd, and observing that the officers were outnumbered and probably not just in persons (weapons too), I quickly realised that this could kick off very nastily and that it was now, all about 'face'.

"Sir, we can talk a little? The youngsters are just excited because I've been away for a while and look, see, they are scared of your men already, and they'll go in soon."

"Lady, I dun tell yuh already, NOW!!" (*"Lady I have told you already, NOW!!"*)

Lukie's party was organised for the next night, my mind in overdrive, I noticed that the verandah was full of crates of beer, I gave Ms. Dulcie a side-look and she nodded.

"Sir I am asking for just a few more minutes, please. Look, your guys seem to be weary and it's hot tonight, why don't you all share a welcome home beer with me, and by the time we're done, the children will be gone?".

He looked at me like I was a crazy lady, nevertheless, with a shrug he cracked a smile, followed by a deep bellowing laugh. With that, he shared out the crate of beers proffered and drove off.

The next day was hectic, old tyre rims filled with coal were placed all around the back yard, soon to be busy frying dumplings, festival, fish and chicken and also boiling rice, rice and peas, yam, banana and dumpling. I sat by the breadfruit tree just absorbing the aromas and anticipating the flavours that only Ms. Tunny could conjure. A multi-talented woman, she could sing (in fact the whole family have incredible voices), and cook unbelievably flavoursome meals. Not a woman to cross too tough though, I have seen her fling a stone around the corner and hit its intended victim, at thirty yards. Having said that, she had a good and compassionate heart.

'Mas George' Miss Tunny's late husband and Danny's father, was a self-taught musician of some repute, and until his death the yard was always full of known and unknown musicians and singers. The children growing there were exposed to every genre of music and musicians, so it was inevitable that Dulcie, Danny, Lukie and his brothers became singers and players of instruments.

The Fire House Crew was born in that yard, Danny and his two friends Paul and George, practiced and rehearsed there together from school days, with Lukie taking lead vocals. A natural comic with a playful sense of humour, Lukie is respected and loved by all within the Reggae industry and within the community.

The party began in earnest. The stage was the gatepost and wall. The upper circle was the Guinep tree. By midnight, the Avenue was packed solid when artistes started passing through to 'toast' the birthday boy. The full L.U.S.T. crew (a popular Jamaican singing group of which Lukie is a member), Beenie Man, Bounty Killer, Dean Fraser, Luciano and a host of young dancehall artistes, kept the party rolling until dawn.

The JCF (Jamaica Constabulary Force) and JDF officers appeared fleetingly to ensure we were all okay after the top half of the Guinep tree gave way to the weight in its branches with a crack and crash, accompanied by shrieks and screams, which were heard way above the music.

Sunday and Monday were reserved for cleaning up and sleeping. It was a good thing that school was in session so at least I rested during the day. Afternoons and evenings of that first week were either spent with the children or in the studios laying tracks with Danny and the rest of the Crew at Steven Stanley Studio and Buju Banton's Gargamel Studio.

Week two, saw me take to the road with Javaughan and Reds again, this time getting to know as much as possible about the real needs of the elders which turned out to be as diverse as the elders themselves.

Miss Bibi, at eighty-six years of age, lived in a timber room measuring twelve feet by twelve feet. The zinc roof was peeling skywards, and everything she owned was jammed neatly into this small space. A large double bedstead, a mattress of sorts, covered in cardboard to create a barrier between springs and occupant, a big old-time fridge, a table and chairs were set up in one corner. A Whatnot and barrels lined the back wall and all were covered with sheets of plastic. Bed, Whatnot and table were always beautifully dressed as only old time Jamaicans can do. You had to walk sideways between everything.

When you stepped in or out and made the mistake of holding on to the side of the doorway, the house creaked and leaned. As much as the interior 'decor' took me nostalgically back to the Jamaican 'front rooms' of the 1960's and 70's (which were only used on Sunday or when they had company), I preferred to chat in the yard.

A fountain of information, I spent many hours over the years talking with Bibi and learning much about the area before and after the 'war'. I learned who was still who in the community, who ran what things and most importantly, who was whose, mother, grandmother, aunty or matriarchal figure in their lives.

I absorbed this information, learning that the running with ballot boxes was NOT a myth. That the arming of men by politicians to control the voting, was NOT a myth. That the raping, looting, murder and mayhem that came with that edict and control was NOT a myth. That the politicians created the don men is NOT a myth and that seven to eight hundred deaths in the run up to the 1980 election is probably pretty conservative.

I learned about the reality of life for so many in the garrison communities and the levels of control over their lives. I also learned who was feuding with whom over what and how long the feud had persisted.

All of this valuable information gave me the tools to later mediate and cool things down when they got heated. Any inter or intra community upsurge would be an excuse to pick up where an old feud left off and to settle old scores. Some feuds went back the full twenty plus years since the 'war', with the sons and even grandsons waiting to exact justice for their loss in those times. The heartfelt cry I heard so many times, "If ongly mi fadda, grandfadda, madda did a live, tings wud a diff'rent fi mi". *("If only my father, grandfather, mother was still alive, things would have been different/better for me".)*

Inspired by Bibi and Javaughan's knowledge, experiences and understanding of the elderly community, I was soon aware of which twenty elders were most in need. I connected with the Trinitarian Church on Delisser Avenue and assisted them in progressing the clearance of documentation with the local relief agency, Food for the Poor (FFP). This ensured our elders were included in the monthly FFP food distribution. Javaughan, Reds and Bibi along with a crew of about eight youngsters (mainly boys) regularly transported these food packages to the elders and in so doing actually created their own home visiting programme.

I travelled back to the U.K. in time to spend Christmas at home with my family in London. I then had the challenge of finding and moving to a smaller dwelling as our six bedroomed local-government apartment was no longer suitable for just me and my son. Mummy and my uncle (who needed life-end care) also required my assistance in ensuring his comfort and well-being in line with their wishes that he remain at home. These events along with other minor events all conspired to deplete my funds and keep me away from Jamaica for over a year. Sad to say, that during my absence Ms. Tunny died, she had been sick for a while, concealing it well. Delisser Avenue would never again feel the same without this woman with the kind and compassionate heart.

Despite the fact that I was busy, the time spent in London provided me with the opportunity to research what was happening worldwide for elders. I discovered that in the Caribbean not only was there an increase in the number of elders, but also an increase in the age to which they now lived. There had been a symposium on Elders at the U.N. in New York and there was a plethora of information at the U.N. Library, disappointingly none of this information was available online at that time. I used the excuse of the research to organise a trip and reconnect with some friends in Connecticut.

NEW YORK

I headed to New York in June 2001, hoping to combine both my research into what policies were being put in place to address the needs of elders, as identified at the recent symposium and my desire to spend a little time on a much-needed catch up with some friends.

I stayed in White Plains and took the train into the city whenever the need arose. I started out at the New York Central Library, an amazing building, so full of history and books of every description and genre imaginable, for a bibliophile like myself, it was heaven. I know that Daddy would also have loved it. The smell of old leather mixed generously with the scent of old beeswax polish, created the impression of walking into the past. The latest information necessary for my research was held at the U.N. Library, therefore, my next stop off.

I entered the famous United Nations building by the public entrance and queued for some time before reaching the security post. Imagine my utter dismay when I was informed that one needed to apply ten days in advance of a visit to make an appointment with the library, for either a half day or a full day. Oh No!! What was I to do? I explained my dilemma that I only had another four days in the U.S.A. and I genuinely needed to access this information to complete my research.

Suddenly, a tiny Asian lady, doll-like, dressed in a white sari, with silvery white hair and standing less than five feet tall, tapped my arm.

"Excuse me, Miss, can I ask what you are researching?"

"Yes ma'am, I would like to find out more about the policies, procedures and recommendations that came out of the recent symposium on elders and elder's care, with a view to collaborating on a project in Jamaica"

"Aah Jamaica, that would be Dr. Eldermire-Shearer's area of expertise, but she's not in New York at the moment, you could contact her at the University in Kingston, I think. Now if you want information from the symposium, then you need to speak to Ms. Carlos. Wait, let me get her extension for you"

With that, she stepped up to the desk, asked for the phone, spoke to someone and handed it over to me. As I took the phone and turned to thank her, she was gone, nowhere to be seen, very eerie!

I spoke with Ms. Carlos who asked me to wait while she came for me. Over the next two days, I was able to meet with the writers of the symposium reports and recommendations. I also met international experts on elders' care, elder activists and people from the inner cities of New York who like me, were just doing whatever they were capable of doing, with what they had available.

Inspired, I returned to London with my new-found knowledge and recommendations. I was determined and invigorated to put the funds together for another Jamaican visit and to help establish a sustainable plan for the golden-agers I had met in Cockburn Pen.

MEETING NEW FOLK

Delisser Avenue did not feel the same without Ms. Tunny or Lukie who had moved out with his young family. So much had changed and the vibes were very different. Ms. Tunny had told everyone that her room, complete with furnishings were mine, however, I knew this would cause contention within the family and decided to look into renting a room elsewhere. At that time, I did not consider moving outside the community, it felt familiar, like home and other than the risk of a stray bullet, I felt safe.

Javaughan greeted me with the sad news that Reds, then the father of a four-month-old son and not yet twenty, had been killed by police in what the police claimed was a shoot-out, just weeks before my return. Javaughan was adamant that the police had shot Reds at point blank range, while still in his bed, they just kicked in the door (his bed was at the side of it) and fired two shots into his chest before he even had the chance to open his eyes properly. Seeing the room and the bed, which had remained untouched as though a monument, it would be hard to dispute Javaughan's version of events.

Undeterred, though saddened, Javaughan gathered the crew together and we made plans for how we would move forward. For the first time, the children's voices were being heard and they were part of the process.

Help with homework was a very high priority, so we set

about finding a tutor to help with Maths and English and of course reading skills.

On the opposite side of Olympic Way, on Henderson Avenue, the St. Margaret's Human Resource Centre is located. It is run by the St Patrick's Foundation which was founded by the lovely Monsignor Richard Albert. After a visit to his office at Stella Maris, we had an agreement whereby I would get a couple of artistes to come and speak to the youth in his programmes and training centres and in return, I could have use of the outside classroom from three p.m. to six p.m. Monday to Friday, term time only. The ever-faithful Dean Fraser, Luciano, Mikey General, alongside another roots reggae singer Warrior King (whose debut single was riding high in the charts), made good on my bargain and between them they continued to do so long after we moved on. For Javaughan and a few of the others, it was the only schooling they had access to. Miss Lorna from Lilly Path, a trained teacher who ran a small 'home school' at her house, was our first tutor.

One evening in mid-November, just after 8 p.m. Dulcie and I were relaxing on the veranda sipping cool coconut water, with a little rum, breaking our peaceful moments there was a commotion on the Avenue and two big SUV's pulled up in front of the yard. A loud, animated young man, in his mid-thirties with a kind of British twang, stepped out of the first vehicle. He was dressed in the latest fashion, sporting some heavy bling and accompanied by what were obviously foot soldiers. He asked to speak to me, I obliged and we went and sat under the breadfruit tree in the back yard with the washing table between us.

"Ms. Myra, I like what you are doing, and I want to help".

Aware that this man was a serious Don both in Jamaica and in London, reputed to be heavily involved in guns and drugs, I would be lying if I said I wasn't somewhat nervous.

"You do? in what way?"

With that, he took a black scandal bag *(carrier bag)* from the foot soldier behind him and slid it across the table. Don't ask me how much was in there, I opened the bag and there were rolls of notes in elastic bands, I didn't stop to count. I closed the bag, tying a knot with the handles and slid it back across the table, quaking inside.

"Sir, thank you very much for the offer, but I can't take it. You and I both know where this has come from and tainted money will taint my work."

I was pretty impressed with my confident outer appearance, which almost faltered when the same youth who had handed him the bag, banged the handle of his gun on the table, shouting

"Yo lady. Who is you? How yuh disrespec di Don so?" *("Hey lady, who do you think you are? How dare you disrespect the Don like that?")*

"Hush bwoy, hush, shi nuh disrepsec mi, mi see a wha. Miss Myra, I respec is where yuh coming from, mi nuh agree wid it, but mi respec it still. If yuh need anyting yuh jus sen one a di yute dem fi mi. Y'hear??" *("Hush boy, hush, she's not being disrespectful, I get what she means. Miss Myra, I see where you are coming from, I don't agree with it, but I respect your decision. If you ever need anything send one of your young people for me. You understand?")*

He shook my hand, hailed Ms. Dulcie and went back to his car driving off with much revving and loud music.

We extended the After-School Club to include the children from Tower Hill. We had two tutors from each Community catering to a total of fifty-four children aged between six and fifteen years.

Also, at this time, I took a daily trot up Olympic Way to the children's home called "My Father's House", run by Mustard Seed Communities on Mahoe Drive, where forty or more children and young people with disabilities reside. I first heard of

Mustard Seed when I carried some special cutlery for the children from one of their London sponsors.

I had heard a lot about the founder of Mustard Seed, Monsignor Gregory Ramkissoon, at that time just Father Gregory, but always "Uncle Father". Knowing of his reputation, having heard people who know him speak in awe of his exploits, his huge spirit and his ability to tap into the good in everyone, I expected to meet a giant of a man. When he came out of his office to greet me, I was astounded to see this lovely, smiling, joyful, rotund and quite short little 'Trini'*(Trinidadian)* man. However, on being hugged by him, Father Gregory has one of the biggest, warmest most congenial spirits I have had the pleasure to meet, it is very easy to overlook his lack of physical stature and see just the giant. He and I have remained close over the years and he has always had my back in a needy situation.

My daily walks up and down Olympic Way were the talk of the communities as I crossed warring turfs, communities at odds with one another and at odds with "Pen" (Cockburn Pen). On opening the gate to me one morning, the guard asked,

"Miss, is true seh yuh live a "Pen?" *(Miss. Is it true you live in Cockburn Pen?)*

"Yes, why?"

"Lady, mi nuh know iffa brave yuh brave, or mad yuh mad!! Yuh really a live deh so an a walk right a wi gates?   Yuh is di ongly s'maddy mi know cum pon foot, in di hole a mi years here." *(Lady, I don't know if you are brave or mad!! You really live there and walk from there to our gates? You are the only person I know who comes here by foot, in all my years here)*

One afternoon, we were playing cricket on Raniford when I was approached by Mikey and Victor, community representatives from Tower Hill who invited us to participate in a youth six a side football tournament.

As President and Vice President of the Tower Hill Progressive League they later brought me across to Tower Hill and introduced me to the elders there in need of help. I was re-introduced to Tower Hill, a place so changed since my visit in 1977, I did not recognise it. Gone were the chicken wire fences, picket gates and that feeling of 'country in town'. In their place, the zinc fences, some of them eight feet high. The league already had good links with Food For the Poor (FFP) and there was a Golden Age club that met regularly at St Paul's Anglican Church. I was also introduced to the incredible Reverend Ernle Gordon, an Anglican priest who has worked and campaigned tirelessly for the disenfranchised.

Another incredible person I met is Frances Madden, a true warrior who has been an inspiration and a firm friend.

Frances was with Grace Kennedy Staff Foundation based at Harbour Street and facilitated a weekly 'round table' meeting of the corner and community leaders to which (with the prior consent of the group), I had been invited. It was fascinating to watch her drawing the best out of these men who were sworn enemies, as she got them, if only for the meeting, to put aside differences and focus on common issues in the Central Kingston area. I learned so much from this amazing, no nonsense, brave and humble woman.

In these meetings, everything was discussed, from how many children from each 'area' were attending the Grace Kennedy homework centre to who was feuding with who, over what, what issues were causing unrest that could lead to violence, to what temporary work would be available through the Christmas, to the Foundation's annual educational scholarships.

Through the meetings facilitated by Francis, I had the opportunity to sit down with men like Broomie, Chubby Dread and Lockie, all notorious political enforcers and 'corner leaders' from Renkers, Tel Aviv and Southside. These men helped enlighten me on the inner thinking of the 'corner leader', his responsibilities (perceived and real) to his turf, his family and his 'bigger heads'.

I was invited by these leaders to come and visit them on their own home turfs and see for myself what they were trying to do. I of course took them up on the offers and spent several days visiting, walking the turfs and speaking to the residents.

For some of these leaders, mainly the younger ones (under thirty), it was an 'opportunity' to show their strength, boasting of exploits and how much they damaged 'the other side', their focus on leaving a legacy of fear. For the older guys, tired of fighting, of watching their peers die out or leave, in the realisation of what is necessary for the younger generation to have a better life, I observed them doing their best to maintain a safe environment. As in all the 'garrison' communities there are rules and repercussions for breaking them, I learned that for the most part, violence was not the first option, but also not something shied away from if felt necessary.

In just six weeks, I had met some incredible people and we had the beginnings of a cross community programme with a listing of over a hundred senior citizens.

2002

ZINC

Having left in January, I was back in Kingston again in March of 2002, this was my last stay at Delisser Avenue. On the plane ride over I read that my friendly Don was shot and killed the previous month on Mountain View Avenue to the East of Kingston. Worthy of a front-page story, the Star newspaper boasted his big bling funeral, glass casket with lights and all sorts.

My return to the Avenue greeted me with the heart-breaking news that young Ricky, the boy with the expressive eyes had been bitten by a dog and the bite became infected. By the time he was taken to hospital some days later, it was too late and he died of blood poisoning.

Not the brightest of starts to the trip.

By the Easter break we had over sixty children in the after-school club and needed to find larger premises. The Tower Hill Progressive League managed the newly opened Tower Hill Community Centre located at St Paul's Anglican churchyard on Tower Avenue.

The churchyard is situated along the gully separating Tower Hill from Cockburn Pen and Waterhouse and runs right out to Waltham Park. On either side of the churchyard were separate intra community turfs with yet two more across the road. There was Top Tower, Middle Tower, Ebony Road, Back Road, Calladium Crescent, Angola, Jah Love Corner, William Crescent and a heap more, all separate turfs. Always heavily armed, with no qualms about fighting and killing one another yet, unbelievably the turfs would unite in an instant against a common enemy! With no single community Don living terribly long, no one wanted the job, so each corner had their own don and they would join forces in times of mutual need.

Had I stopped to think about the risks involved in working in that environment with those dynamics, I would probably have turned back to London and spent any future trips to Jamaica in an all-inclusive on the North Coast. But I didn't as unwittingly I stepped out in the Christian Faith I professed and stepped into my purpose.

My friendship with Ms. Bibi enabled me to communicate on a different level with the corner dons, although she lived in Cockburn Pen, her history and friendships stretched far and wide. Bibi and her late husband (who she only ever referred to as Dada) were political activists, she a staunch PNP supporter and he a strong JLP activist, he tall and broad, she petite. I can imagine there being some very colourful exchanges between them near election time. Childhood sweethearts, they married in their teens and in spite of their political differences, lived a happy, peaceful life. They only had one child, Marcus, who died of a 'fever' in 1962, only five years old.

Just days before the 1980 election, Dada was 'taken' from outside the yard gate and found the following morning in the gully bound in rope, a single shot to the head and 'tagged' with a piece of cardboard tied around his neck on which was drawn a bell, a sign that he was a JLP supporter. Even though they were likely responsible for Dada's murder, Bibi remained loyal to her party and continued to live in the little one room house Dada and she built together after Marcus died.

At the invitation of the Progressive League, we moved our

'operations' into the Community Centre hosting an Easter Art Competition. I was able to ensure that a personal invitation was made to each individual leader to submit an entry from their turf and the panel of judges included the matriarchs of several main turfs.

At that time, it was not possible to get the guys all together in one space, so a heap of walking up and down was involved.

In May we had very heavy rainfalls which saturated the homes of many of the elders. Along with the Progressive League and their community videographer, I toured the community interviewing the elders about their needs and showing the conditions of their dwellings. Mr. Thomas, the Principal of Seward Primary and All Age School on Olympic Way proposed that we show them the video at a meeting with him and Bruce Bicknell of Tankweld Steel. Subsequently, Mr. Bicknell donated a tonne of thirteen-foot sheets of zinc and a tonne of twelve-foot sheets which would provide protection from the weather to the elders most in need. Mindful that a needs assessment had to be conducted properly, I requested that they hold the zinc until such time as this was completed and we were ready to distribute it, hopefully, within a week.

I did the walk from Three Mile to Bay Farm Road, assessing with the corner leaders, which of the elders were the wettest, the oldest and had the least support. Finally, with a list that included elders from the length and breadth of Olympic Way, every single sheet of zinc was allocated and we had only touched those seventy-five-years and older! I showed the final list to each of the corner men and where requested, showed them the room or section to be covered. They all seemed happy with the choices made and this new way of participating in the decision-making process, instead of their previous method of working (hands on, take your portion first and grab what you can). All, except one. And you will always find one!

His name was Bigs. He came to the office on day three of the assessments wanting to know where his portion of zinc was.

I told him he was not in the age group we were catering to at this time.

Three more times Bigs came to the office to inquire as to his portion of zinc only to be turned away with the same response. Day five, he sat across the desk from me and pulled out a nine-millimeter semi-automatic gun, placed it on the table between us and patted the butt.

"So Ms Myra, yuh really a guh tell mi seh mi nah get nuh zinc?" (*"So, Miss Myra, you're really going to tell me that you won't give me the zinc?"*)

Looking slightly snootily down my nose at the gun, I pushed it back across the desk and bluffed.

"Oh please. Is that supposed to frighten me? Cho. I knew the Kray's and all the East End and the Essex gangsters, we ate bigger guns than that for breakfast when you were still in short pants".

Truth is, I had gone to school with two (distant) members of the Kray family and several daughters of Essex gangsters, but didn't 'know' their families per se and the only guns we ate were sweetie ones.

Reaching into my pocket, I took out a five hundred Jamaican dollar note and slid it across the table.

"Look, if you are that desperate for a sheet of zinc, take this up to Mr. Dabdoub at Budget, tell him I sent you and can you please get two sheets of zinc at my discount, but you're not having any of my elders' zinc."

Had he been able to see through the desk, Bigs would have seen my legs shaking uncontrollably despite the cool façade that appeared from the waist up.

I searched Bigs' face to see if maybe I had gone too far, trying valiantly to control the shaking that threatened to take over my whole body.

First a snort, then a twitch followed by a roaring laugh that seemed to shake the whole building.

"Mi nuh guh call yuh Ms Myra again, yuh is now di Iron Lady, y'hear?" *(I'm not going to call you Ms Myra anymore, you are now the Iron Lady, alright?)*

With that, he pocketed the note and left the centre, gun resting on his shoulder and you could hear him laughing all the way up Tower Avenue.

It took me a moment or two to process what had just happened and to control my legs enough to stand and head straight for the bathroom where I must have lost twenty pounds down the pan. An effective though not recommended, weight loss moment.

We were ready for collection and distribution of the zinc, nails and lumber that had all been donated. I got a call from Tankweld Steel to meet Mr. Bicknell at the centre early on Saturday morning where he surprised us with an additional tonne of zinc on behalf of the local political representative. He asked that we distribute it within the same criteria as we had with the rest and to guarantee it would not be used 'politically'. I gave my word. The rest of Saturday was spent batching up the zinc into the allocations, by the community and then by street and number. The additional zinc was put to one side and the corner men from Back Road, St Paul's Lane /Ebony Road, William Crescent and Tamarind Turn agreed to watch the churchyard and see that everything remained untouched.

On Sunday I arrived at St Paul's with Javaughan around six a.m., where we met several of the League members and corner leaders. We checked off the inventory, all was in order and by eight a.m. there was a steady stream of vehicles coming to collect materials.

Suddenly from out of nowhere, the churchyard seemed dominated with people demanding zinc. A few of the corner leaders and Dons moved to the front of the building and a few remained inside standing behind me. The crowd of about forty or fifty was getting quite boisterous in its demands, and I could feel another weight loss moment coming on.

As we argued back and forth for what seemed like ages but was, in fact, less than sixty seconds, I was enraged by the fact that these people knew this was for the elders and still wanted to take it for their own selfish reasons, either to use or to sell. Standing in the middle of the doorway, hands on my hips, I drew up every inch of my five-foot four-inch height and I yelled (in temper).

"If any of you feel say you are going to get any of this here zinc, know say you will have to take me out first!!!"

I am not sure if I actually closed my eyes as I heard the click-click of safeties on the guns, but I could see Daddy before me as on numerous occasions, hands on shaking head, pulling at the little hair he had left, "Jaysus Mary and Joseph, you and your mouth. Sure you'd make a fine diplomat one of these days, sure you would, were it not for your mouth".

As I returned to the moment in hand, I realised that it was the corner leaders and Dons who were cocking their guns ready to defend me if necessary. The crowd dispersed quickly and quietly and as if by magic, the guns disappeared into thin air. Exit left rear to the bathroom.

Not a weight loss regime I would recommend but everyone was truly impressed with my slender figure when I returned to London at the end of May.

The last few days before I returned to London to see the family, were spent checking the repairs and the materials used, taking photographs of the completed repairs and I signed off on over forty roofs, submitting the documented list to Tankweld Steel.

Two days after the distribution I was approached by Patrick a local crack-head whilst walking on Olympic Way. His baby-mother had received ten sheets of zinc as instructed and supplied by Mr. Bicknell separately and which were installed by the community team. Patrick appeared very jittery and obviously seeking his next hit.

"Ms Myra, wi need more zinc yuh know." *(Ms Myra, we need more zinc you know!)*

"Really? I know we completely covered your baby-mother's room. What happened?"

"Look like is tief dem tief di roof'" *(It looks like someone stole the roof")*

"Sorry about that, but I can't help you with any more zinc, you had your allocation"

"But dem tief it!!!!" *("But they stole it")*

"I don't think so Patrick, I hear say it was you took off the zinc and sold them over White Wing and Belrock"

With that he flew into a rage, stomped up and down threateningly, cussing me out royally and citing a litany of what he would do to me if he didn't get his zinc. I walked off cussing under my breath, "Blasted crackhead Patrick, who the hell he thinks he is threatening??"

The following day I moved from Delisser Avenue into a rented room in a family yard on Phillipo Avenue, with Ms. Esmee, Mas Peter and family, (in-laws to Miss Tunny). I thought no more of the incident until I saw Patrick, leaning up against a light-post the next day as I was leaving for London, his left arm and right leg in plaster and his face rather battered.

"Is yuh cause dis yuh know!!!" he shouted at me. *("You caused this you know!!!")*

"Me??? How you work that out?"

"A nuh yuh a tell di man dem seh mi a trouble yuh??" *("Wasn't it you told the dons I was harassing you?)*

"Me?? I never told anyone anything."

And I really hadn't, apparently, I didn't mumble quietly enough. The incident had been observed by one of the 'corner youth' who made a report to his 'boss' that whatever was said between me and Patrick had upset me because I just passed him cussing under my breath and hadn't even hailed him and I always hailed him before. 'Boss' was upset that I had been distressed and decided Patrick needed to be taught a lesson.

I learned one too, keep the grumbling and cussing until you reach home or others may get hurt, some undeservedly.

TEACHER

During my time in London I relaxed with family and fairly successfully, begged resources and finance to return to Kingston for the first 'Unity Summer Camp'.

What a tricky time it was coordinating the bringing together of children from across warring communities. That first Unity Summer Camp in July 2002 would be the first time in decades, the children from these communities, would all be together in one space outside of school!

I chose to ignore the usual separations across the community. I went to Top Tower, Bottom Tower and in between, Bay Farm Villa, Compound, Mall Road, Cockburn Pen pulling together over one hundred children ensuring that I included at least one child from the families of each of the local corner men, Dons and community leaders, which I figured was one way of mitigating any violence during Camp hours. I spent a week working with the youth from the local Marching Band, training them to be teaching assistants, making resources and teaching aids.

As Camp opened up, children literally two and three years of age turned up, mainly as they were being cared for by older siblings whilst mummy, grandma or even great-grandma, looked about 'back to school' (preparing for new school year). What was I going to do with these babies? We had use of the Church, the Basic School and the Centre, so we moved the babies into one class area of the basic school.

There was one corner youth named Damon, who had no family of the ages for Camp and could potentially pose a bit of a problem as his lack of literacy skills made him unpredictable. As far as he saw, everyone was 'getting' something out of the programme except him and he was feeling uncomfortable about it.

Damon was nineteen or twenty years old, eyes as cold as steel, a temper that was quick and could be fatal, definitely not a man to cross. Clad as usual in slippers, mesh merino and cut-off jeans with one leg rolled up, he watched me with the baby-class. I saw him slide in beside Kimo (four years old), who was singing the alphabet. Damon joined in the singing and I saw him smile for the first time in the two years I had known him, a real, genuine smile. I sent the little ones into the playground to await lunch and called Damon over into the office.

"Damon, you know I am really swamped. I can't be in the classroom with the babies and on the road getting food and stuff for the children, you could help me out?"

"Miss Myra, yuh dun know seh mi cyaan read" ("Miss Myra, you already know that I can't read")

"But you don't need to, just sing them their ABC, 123, play two games and kick two balls with them, it would really help me out."

The following morning Damon turned up, on time, in his usual attire. I didn't mention this, just his presence was enough for me and his willingness to do me a favour. At the end of the day he brought us both a cold Red Stripe (local beer) and sat with me in the office, a smile on his face like you rarely see from anyone, it lit up the whole room, sipping on his beer, he looked at me and said,

"Mi know wha mi a go do tomorrow, dem nice, tanks y'hear", got up and left. ("I know what I'm going to do tomorrow, they are nice, thanks, you hear?")

Wednesday, Damon arrived punctually, but this time, dressed in black church pants, polished black church shoes, white merino under a pressed shirt and a smile. I was a little surprised, to say the least, I smiled back.

"Is wha Miss Myra?" *("What you looking at Miss Myra?")*

"I'm just loving the look."

"So wha'ppen, yuh nuh seh mi a teacher?" *("So what's wrong, didn't you say I am a teacher?")*

"Well, yes"

"So, mi nuh fi look like a one?" *("So, shouldn't I look like one?")*

"I am impressed".

At the end of Camp, when he received his Certificate of Appreciation and a framed picture of him and his class, he hugged me up tight.

"Miss Myra, yuh dun know. Seriously tho' yuh see when di pickney dem look pon mi, hands up an a please sir, please sir, is different, dem don't scared, dem love mi an respec mi, Jah know seh is different!!". *("Miss Myra, you know how it goes. Seriously though, when the children look up at me, hands up, please sir, please sir, it feels different, they're not scared of me, they love me and respect me, God knows it feels different!!")*

Not for the first, nor the last time, I had to rush to the bathroom before the tears could gush.

JUST A LITTLE HIKE
BLUE MOUNTAIN

T he Band's youth and I got pretty close, so when they asked if I would chaperone them for a "little hike" because their parents wouldn't let them go without one, I agreed.

On Friday evening at myself and twenty young people aged between twelve and twenty years gathered at St Paul's and climbed aboard the bus chartered to take us to Mavis Bank which sits above Kingston, at the foot of the Blue Mountains where we were to start the hike. I suppose I have to take some responsibility for the fact that I didn't research the trip! Most unwise. My summation, which was totally incorrect, was that as we were arriving after dark, it is unlikely we would be hiking far. In fact, I was assured (totally falsely) that it was just a couple of hours. Quite forgetting this is Jamaica and there is no real sense of time here, I accepted the assertion of a couple of hours.

By the time we reached Mavis Bank, it was already dark and only just within the hours of entry. Our guide, a senior band member named Errol, took the list of hikers over to the Police Station and we were given the all clear to start our hike. All this rigmarole should have alerted me that something was not quite as originally presented.

We began our ascent, not too bad at first, bit rocky, couldn't see too far ahead, but it was a clear night with a bright moon lighting our way, we all managed to stay in sight of one another but the scenery was hidden. I was told we were heading to a campsite and duly shepherded the youngsters along the way, again the thought struck me that I should have researched. We sang old school reggae, church choruses and dancehall classics as we trudged the first couple of hours.

"So, Errol, is how far now?"

"Oh Miss Myra, is jus di otha side a di river!!" *("Oh Miss Myra, it's just the other side of the river!!")*

Now if you had heard the sincerity with which those words were uttered, you would have believed, as I did, that we were near the river, and that there was only one. No!! In fact, we trudged at least another hour to the first one.

Finally, we reached the river please don't ask me which one, a river on the way up Blue Mountain. And at that precise moment, the moon is covered by one of the few clouds of the night.

"Errrmmm, Errol, I don't see any bridge"

"Oh yes, Miss Myra is a bamboo one, we walk pon one and hold on pon di otha, is just up here" *("Oh yes Miss Myra, there's a bamboo one, you walk on one and hold onto the other, it's just up there")*

We inched up a little further and yes there it was, the river could not be seen but only heard at this point. The youngsters happily made their way across, so I felt assured that all was fine. I executed the crossing by sliding my feet along the bottom bamboo while holding on to the top one, confidently too I might add. On reaching the other side I jumped down off the bamboo as I had seen the youngsters do, I missed the bank which resulted in soaked shoes, socks and feet. I now had to complete the ascent in wet trainers and socks.

The journey got very painful as the rubbing of the footwear produced blisters and by the time we completed the hike there were huge holes in my heels. We trudged for what seemed like hours to the next river, which bless their hearts, the boys carried me over.

"Errol, how far now?",

"Is not too far, is jus Jacob's Ladder to go" *("It's not too far now, it's just Jacob's Ladder to go")*

Again, a warning sign totally ignored, Jacob's Ladder?! Now I know a little Bible so I should have taken note. I should have remembered this is Jamaica where "soon come", means anything but, "just a few chains", could actually be miles and "not too far", was in fact very, very far, even as the crow flies.

Most of our ascent to this point had been on tracks and narrow roadways. As we approached the foot of Jacob's Ladder, the road was wider and I saw a jeep drive up and stop at the bar by the side of the road, two couples and what appeared to be a local guide, got out, bid the driver a thank you and headed off in front of us onto the Ladder.

"Errol, please tell me they are an illusion, I am dreaming?"

"Oh no Miss Myra, is not a dream, yuh know say wi coulda drive right up here, an jus do di Ladder? fi real, would a easier, don't?" *("Oh no Miss Myra, it's not a dream, do you know that we could have driven right up to here and just do the Ladder for real, it would have been easier, isn't that right?")*

I just looked at him, open mouthed, living eye water streaming down my face as I looked up at what seemed insurmountable. Errol and Javaughan hugged me up,

"Hush, Miss Myra, wi a guh help yuh" *("Hush Miss Myra, we're going to help you")*

Where it was possible to do so, the bigger boys paired up and "chaired" me and where only one could pass, they made a cradle across my back with their arms and inched me across safely. Finally, in the early morning hours, we reached the cabins. Sharing the sheets some had remembered to pack, most stretched out to sleep, some inside, some on the veranda and others heading off to Nanny's Lookout to watch the sun rise.

We managed to keep everyone amused, fed and safe, I did

nothing but try to fix my heels which had deep, painful holes rubbed into them. My Jamaican First Aid Kit proved to be most helpful, a capful of Dettol to wash out the sore, a hefty pouring of Peroxide to sterilize and seal it, Aloe gel, generously applied on cotton and tied in place with a bandage, changed hourly.

Sunday five a.m., everyone was up and packed, ready to start our descent, my feet, cushioned by the cotton pads, able to walk a little better and much less painfully.

At this stage I must impart some vital information. I have a real fear of heights and have difficulty even looking down a flight of stairs. I can't honestly tell you how beautiful the scenery was all the way down only the bit that had wider pathways and roads. I scrambled over the first of a number of landslides, realising that one slip could mean a sheer drop of tens of feet and in some places, looked like, hundreds of feet. A mixture of both horror and pride struck me as I realised we had traversed these same landslides on the way up, in the pitch darkness of the predawn hours. With that thought in mind, I clung, face to the mountainside, for the most part of the descent.

On reaching what was now the second river, we sat in the rock pools, and the youngsters splashed and romped.

"Errol, I don't see where we crossed the other night, why didn't we cross here?"

"Yuh cyaan cross dis a night, di river don't stable an can wash yuh away, di bridge deh deh behin yuh" *("You can't cross this at night, the river isn't stable and cash wash you away, the bridge is up there behind you")*

Yes indeed, there it was, right on the edge of the waterfall, one false move or slip could have ended very nastily.

When we reached Mavis Bank, I looked across and up to the hills and knew with all certainty in my heart, that had it been daylight, had I seen where we were going, had I researched the hike, even if we had boarded the bus maybe we would have stopped for supper in Mavis Bank, but we would definitely have turned right back to Tower Hill. God knows why He let me do the ascent at night.

When I met with the youth on Monday ready to lambast them for my pain and suffering, the joy they expressed at having made the trip, the fun and laughter they were having, during the meeting, was infectious and all I could do was laugh with them.

During the weekend, we had jokes, we had serious reasonings about the reality of their lives, their aspirations and they made me feel very special for having gone with them. I understood more and more about the critical turning points in the lives of young people in Jamaica's inner city. I felt privileged that they had the confidence to talk about parts of their lives that brought them to where they were, good and bad. I realized I had a very special relationship with many of them and to this day when we meet up anywhere, the first thing out of their mouths after "How are you?" is:

"Member when wi go a Blue Mountain, how wi trick yuh seh it don't far?" ("*Remember when we went to Blue Mountain, how we tricked you that it wasn't far*")

MARCHING BAND

A number of the young people assisting with Unity Summer Camp were members of the local marching band. They had instruments, but not uniforms, material for which had been promised by a local entity but never appeared.

We arranged some metal cans for collecting donations. Over a two-day period, the band members embarked on a 'walkathon' and stood at traffic lights up and down Kingston rattling their cans and soliciting funds. When they were finished Kizzy, (an eighteen year old mum of a three year old child) and Errol (one of the band's leaders) brought the tins which we then opened, sorted and counted. 'Orange' money to one side, piles of one and five Jamaican dollar coins, even more of, ten and twenty-dollar coins, a significant number of fifty dollar notes some one hundred-dollar notes and even a five hundred note. The grand total they had collected was nine thousand, four hundred and sixty Jamaican dollars and some copper. Purchasing enough material for a troupe of twenty dancers and eighteen players of instruments, was going to be a challenge.

The Band's members agreed on blue for the main colour with white and yellow inserts. The local tailor estimated the material requirements for twenty skirts, eighteen pairs of pants and thirty-eight jackets at four bolts blue, two white and two yellow. That's a pretty tall order on our budget when a single bolt starts at four thousand Jamaican dollars.

Four of the band members and I went off to LP Azar, (the big fabric importer and wholesaler in Crossroads). I was able to speak directly with the lovely Mr. Peter Azar and when I explained what we wanted and what funding we had available you could almost hear his mental calculator at work.

I wasn't too sure (having just met the man) if the twitch in the corner of his mouth was one of annoyance or amusement. The twitch spread into a smile, then a chuckle and we had a conversation about where I was at, as he put it, "serving Jamaica" and wasn't I aware of the dangers of "those kinds of areas". He agreed that we could have the fabric, on the proviso that we wait until after lunch to collect it as they observed a strict lunch hour, whereby all business ceases.

I had to leave the band members to go sort out other business and asked them to wait patiently as Mr. Azar had agreed to help us, but at the moment he's busy. I gave Kizzy the receipt for the material and money for patty and juice for the four of them and headed off. When I got back to the centre I expected to see Kizzy and the others back with their fabric but had to wait until after six p.m. for them to appear.

"Whatever took you guys so long, are you OK?"

"Yes Ms Myra, wi did a wait pon Missa Azar" (*"Yes Miss Myra, we were waiting for Mr. Azar*)

"So long?"

"Yes Ms Myra, is true say im well busy, so wi did jus wait like yuh seh til im done" (*"Yes Miss Myra, it's true he is very busy, so we just waited like you said until he was finished"*)

"An is near closing im member wi. Is like im did forget, but wi was patient. Missa Azar said you fi call im" (*"It was near closing when he remembered us. It's like he forgot, but we were patient. Mr. Aar asked for you to call him"*)

Now if you knew this crew like I did, patience is not a virtue displayed by any one of them, much less when together. I was very impressed with them, even more so after I spoke with Mr. Azar, who said at first, he forgot they were there, then as he remembered and went to deal with them, he was called into the office so they were left standing. When he came out to sort out the fabric, the crew was still quietly waiting where he left them, he was so impressed with how patiently and politely they waited for him for well over two hours that he gave them an extra bolt of the blue fabric.

At the end of the summer, Mr. Azar donated six dozen sets of khaki uniforms enabling seventy-two boys, aged six to fourteen years to start the upcoming school year with at least one new uniform.

UNITY SUMMER CAMP

That first Unity Summer Camp in 2002 turned out to be a truly, rip roaring success, commencing early July (school breaks up first Friday of July) and bringing together outside of mainstream school, for the first time in over thirty years, children from across the political divides of Kingston 11, from Three Miles to Seaward Drive, Spanish Town Road to Waltham Park Road.

The enmities that divided these communities ran deep and through each new generation. The first day of Camp the children maintained a distance from one another in 'community' cliques, it was apparent that a number were armed with stones, pieces of pipe and pieces of board. As we went through pockets and checked trouser legs, I came across a little girl six years old (whose daddy was a corner Don), armed with a small plastic soda bottle containing a crushed Scotch Bonnet pepper in vinegar.

"Little Miss, where are you going with that"

"Hey Lady, mi haffi tek care yuh know" *("Hey lady, I have to take care you know")*

"Take care from what?"

"Lady, if dem deh Pen pickney feel seh dem can trouble mi, dem fi tink again. Mi a go bun out dem y-eye wid dis!" *("Lady, if the Cockburn Pen children think they can trouble me, they can think again. I will burn out their eyes with this!")*

She maintained her big bad attitude until I said we would go and have a word with Daddy to ensure there was no repeat of the arming up. We found out later that she had demanded things in the local shops, in her father's name, while he, poor thing, was totally unaware, and no one wanted to complain to him because he was not the most stable of folk and could flip at any time. I found I was able to communicate well with this don, and the vast majority of corner men and dons I met, by addressing, not the don, but the young lad Grandma took to Sunday School, because he lurks there waiting for a safe opportunity to show himself, the 'good s'maddy' *(the good person)*.

The first week of Camp we were breaking up fights at the rate of two or three an hour, the vast majority, a result of the hostilities and prejudices of the adults in their lives. By the end of week two, we were down to one or two a day then eventually fighting amongst them became a rare occurrence.

UNITY SUMMER CAMP DAY TRIP

Towards the end of Camp, we commandeered a few local route mini-buses and made a trip to Ital Spring in Caymanas, St Catherine, with swimming, crispy fried sprats and festival, cold bag juice, everyone having the most enjoyable time, splashing, playing and eating. The corner men had ensured they each had a 'soldier' on duty to watch out for their family members on the trip. I sat chatting with a couple of the foot soldiers, one a young man in his late teens, the other a middle-aged man in his late forties-early fifties who just kept staring around him and smiling to himself.

"What's up Dread?"

"Nuttin, jus' tekin' it een." (*"Nothing, just taking it all in"*)

"You look like you haven't seen country in a long time"

"Yuh right, mi don't lef' the Avenue (Tower Avenue) since di 'lection war days" (*"You're right, I haven't left the Avenue since the election war days"*)

"What? From 1980 seriously??"

"Is before dat, '79. Dem kill fi mi baby-madda, all a rape an' a bun har. All now mi cyaan pass a jerk pan an don't feel sick. Bun up pork and bun up s'maddy smell di same, yuh did know?" (*"Since before that, 1979. They killed my baby-mother, all raped and then burnt her. All now I can't pass a jerk pan and don't feel sick. Charred pork and charred human smell the same, did you know that?")*

"Mi di 'affi go find dem deh dutty bwoy, a mi an Grumpy find dem, di four a dem. Mi say mi a guh mek dem feel it like mi baby-madda. Wi did chop chop dem, nuh fi kill dem, jus mek dem hurt an bleed. Wen dem bleed out weaky weaky, we jus drop two tire 'pon dem, an drop dem body inna di pig-pen. Is from dem times deh, mi a mind de pig pen fi nuff man, mi affi keep low.... Yuh know seh pig nyaam di bone too? Long time mi nuh go a river or beach, is pretty, don't?" *("I had to go find those dirty boys. Grumpy and I found them, the four of them. I said I was going to make them feel it like my baby-mother did. We chopped them [with machetes], not to kill them outright, just to make them hurt and bleed. When they were weak from loss, we just lit up two tires on them and dropped their bodies in the pig pen. It's from those times there I have looked after the pig pens for enough of the Dons and have to keep low. You know that pigs eat the bones too? Long time since I've been to the river or beach, it's pretty here, isn't it?")*

I had long learned to mask any feelings of shock or horror at some of the things I saw or heard or the speed with which the subject changes as though what was said is of no consequence.

Over a hundred children enjoyed the day with not a single accident or incident.

UNITY SUMMER CAMP
- THE LAST WEEK

Mark was a Rasta youth from Villa then in his early thirties, a community activist, respected by all and a community 'gatekeeper', able to cross all territories, cognizant of who was who, who needed help, who was aligned to which don, corner man or politician because he was aligned to none. He attached himself to the Camp and proved to be a great asset over the years, accessing children and elders in need across the communities and often accompanied Javaughan and me on the many 'begging' trips to wholesalers, stores, manufacturers and suppliers of everything, in search of what the Camp needed.

Nicky was twenty-one years old with two children six and two years old. She attached herself to me on my first visits to Tower Hill, she had basic administration skills, loved dance and drama and was not a bad little singer. She became my P.A. for the next ten years and walked every step of the streets with me.

The last week was spent getting ready for the Camp Closing Ceremony, each 'class' preparing its own item of song, dance or recitation. Mark, Javaughan and I spent the week collecting, exercise books, backpacks, pens, pencils, markers, khakis, underwear, socks, merinos (vests), donated and hugely discounted by LP Azar, BASHCO, Lerner Stores, Kingston Bookshop and Sangster's Bookshop to name but a few.

Finally, the big day arrived, the Church filled with parents, family and onlookers from across the communities, each one eager to see their child perform. The children entered in pairs, every one of them dressed in their 'Sunday' best, carrying a candle held through a piece of card singing the gospel song "Carry your candle, go light your world".

For two and a half hours in between presentations of backpacks filled with back to school goodies, the children entertained their parents, families and friends with renderings from Miss Lou, Classic Reggae, Gospel songs, original skits and dances of every kind. Every child received a certificate for attendance with their back pack and additionally special certificates of achievement for Kindness and Courtesy to Others, Most Polite, Most Helpful, First in Maths, English, Reading and Most Improved Behaviour, were awarded to outstanding attendees.

All of the 'teachers' received a Certificate of Appreciation and a framed photograph of their class.

I was presented with a large bottle of Rum Cream, a huge gift basket full of all kinds of sweets and chocolates and the 'teachers' serenaded me with a beautiful rendition of "The Wind Beneath My Wings", which of course made me cry.

One of the things I had noticed at the Camp, was the numbers of children who were in the care of elderly guardians who appeared, for the most part, to be their sole providers, several of these primary care givers were on our list of elders in need!! I found this very disturbing.

2003

LEARNING TO DUCK

I left Kingston in October 2002 for a prolonged visit with family in the UK and returned in April 2003 to my rented room on Phillipo Avenue just two minutes from Delisser Avenue, round by Mas. Peter and Miss Esmee, family to Ms Tunny.

I had arrived very late the previous night and being over-tired, couldn't sleep. I took a walk round to Ms. Dulcie for an early morning coffee and we sat on the veranda waiting for the sun rise, catching up on the happenings in my absence. Dance-hall music was playing in the distance, from more than one direction.

A movement across the bottom of the road caught my eye, a bit early for a man to be on the road, a bit late for 'changing of the guard', besides, there appeared to be three or four people in the gloom on the edge of Raniford.

Suddenly a barrage of gunshot rained across Raniford, semi-automatic or automatic weapons by the sounds, but I didn't hang about outside to check visually. After what seemed for-ever, but was probably less than sixty seconds, everything went quiet, except for the dancehall music still playing in the dis-tance. People gathered in the street, Dulcie and I went to the gate to find out what had happened. The three or four people I thought I saw earlier turned out to be six, Javaughan amongst them. The only time I ever saw him armed.

Now, five foot four inches is not a lot of height, but, fill it with a mixture of Irish temper and 'done with the foolishness, do what you will' attitude, I am told, it becomes quite awesome, even scary. Was I shaking with anger or fear? Both probably, but mainly anger. As I saw Javaughan among the gunmen I called his name, he looked around seeing me at the gate. With almost magical speed, the AK's and the M16's disappeared behind backs.

I was reminded of the old Laurel and Hardy or Three Stooges movies as the guys kind of side stepped across the front of the gate looking a bit sheepish, (two actually on tiptoe,) with their rifle muzzles extending above their heads. "Mawnin' Miss Myra". As he passed me Javaughan leaned in, "Sorry Miss Myra, we neva know seh yuh home!!" *("Sorry Miss Myra, we never knew you had come home [to Jamaica]!!")*

As they moved up the road, it was hard not to laugh as they grumbled between them, still holding their weapons with the muzzles above their heads, this time in front of them.

"Mi neva kno seh shi deh" *("I never knew she was here")*

"'Ow mi fi kno?" *("How would I know?")*

"Same way coulda man fi kill wi, wi fi kno who inna di place" *("Just the same, could have been someone coming to kill us, we have to know who is in the place")*

"Di dods nuh guh like seh wi wake har up yuh kno" *("The Don isn't going to like that we woke her up you know")*

"Bwoy yuh si fi har face, lawd mi sarry fi har pickney dem" *("Boy, did you see her face, Lord I'm sorry for her children")*

"Javaughan, yuh nuh see seh shi ready fi lick yuh like shi a yuh granny." *("Javaughan, didn't you see how she was ready to slap you like she's your granny?")*

When he came to see me later in the day, Javaughan apologised for the incident earlier, explaining that it had been a reprisal attack for a drive-by a few days previously which they believed had been perpetrated by Back Road. By the end of the day,

I realised I had come home to war raging on both inter and intra community fronts.

I spent a lot of time with Bibi that week as she filled me in on all the happenings during my absence. With Mark and Nicky in tow, we visited all the matriarchal figures of influence from Three Mile to Seaward Drive, seeking solutions to some of what was going on.

One of the intra-community feuds had been going on for over twelve years. In that time, seven people were dead and another eleven injured. Through the mother of one and the aunt of the other, I requested a meeting to talk about their problem and see if we could come to a non-violent solution.

A couple of days later I received a call to say the meeting was agreed and I was 'sent for' after midnight. Escorted by 'foot soldiers' from both sides of the feud, I made my way out to Olympic Way and down to Seaward School, considered neutral territory. The watchman opened the gate and ushered us to the tree beside the gate where there were three chairs (probably from the school staff room), arranged in a triangle, to the back of the tree. I could see this as a good thing in that the high walls to the back and side of the chairs, and the tree to the front would be a good cover but on the other hand, there was nowhere to run if it became necessary.

The two men arrived, both in their early to mid-forties, beer bellies and each obviously trying to outdo the other in both bling and 'style' (which would have better suited young men half their age and size). A card table was set up between us and furnished with a large bottle of Wray & Nephew overproof rum, three bottles of Ting, a cooking pot filled with ice and a pack of disposable cups. It looked like this was going to be some night.

As the 'matriarch' of the meeting I was asked to say a prayer before we started, so we stood, held hands and I prayed two prayers, one silently that went along the lines of:

"Lord please let me get out of this in one piece, uninjured. I know I put myself in these positions, and I promise to stop and think before I act, but I wouldn't do it without the faith that You will carry me safely through (I hope) again."

My lips however uttered a slightly different:

"Lord, take us through this night in peace and safety, may your sons find a solution to their anger, in Jesus' name, Amen"

What I have learned and have said many times is, no matter how deviant the man, inside there is (in the majority), the boy grandma took to Sunday school and over the years it has been the corner man, the don and bad-man that have insisted every meeting open with a prayer.

As we sat back down, one of the 'soldiers' set up four cups with hefty portions of rum, three with ice, the first without, which was then dribbled around us in a circle, a libation to please the spirits of the dead, apparently.

I poured as much Ting into the cup as it would take and sipped it gently as the men swigged theirs down rather quickly and another silent prayer went up:

"Lord, please let them be happy drunks, not miserable or violent ones, Amen".

We exchanged a few pleasantries over their first drink and then it was down to business.

"What is going on with you guys? You live in the same community, barely three streets separate you and yet there's this constant madness."

"A fi'im fault, is 'im start eet" *("It's his fault, he started it")*

"A lie dat, is yuh an yuh cousin" *(That's a lie, it was you and your cousin")*

"Who wants to take it from the beginning for me?"

"Is fi' 'im people dem kill Marco" *("It was his people who killed*

Marco")

"So wha, unnu neva shoot up Freddie an Blue?" (*"So what, didn't you shoot up Freddie and Blue?"*)

"But a nuh dem mash up Bernie yard?" (*"But wasn't it they who destroyed Bernie's place?"*)

"That's all since I've known you, what happened in the beginning?"

"Mi di guh a prison, six year mi deh a GP (General Penitentiary, Kingston) an den mi win mi h'appeal fi come a road. Is when mi deh a GP 'bout year an likkle bit mi find seh mi baby-madda a gi mi bun wid fi im fambily. Dat bad enough, but dem deh inna mi yard!! Dem fi guh a one 'otel, dem don't s'posed to be inna mi bed!! So, mi sen mi nephew fi guh talk to di yute". (*"I went to prison, spent six years in GP and won my appeal for freedom. When I was there just over a year I found my baby-mother was having an affair with his family member. That was bad enough but they were together in my house!! They should have gone to a hotel, they shouldn't be in my bed!! So, I sent my cousin to talk to the youth".*)

"But 'im neva 'affi beat di yute like dat. A piss bag 'im a walk wid from then Miss Myra, dat don't fair." (*But they never had to beat the youth like that. He's had to walk with a urine bag since then*)

"But is unnu cum kill mi nephew. An 'im a mi sista one bwoy, har wash belly too, so yuh dun kno' 'ow dat a guh go!!" (*But your people killed my nephew. And he's my sister's one boy, her last child too, so you have to know how that will go!!*)

The list of grievances went on, who shot who, who chopped who, back and forth, tit for tat. By the time they finished relating the twelve years of feuding, I was on my second rum but lagging way behind the men who were about to open a flask of Appleton's Special having finished the Wray, aware now that my third prayer had been heard. They seemed quite jolly.

Having related their stories they looked at me,

"So, Miss Myra, is wha yuh seh?" (*"So Miss Myra, what say you?"*)

"Really? One question though. Where is your baby-mother now, are you still together?"

"No sah, is long time wi dun, shi an mi bwoy deh a farrin, years." *("No, we finished long ago, she and my son are overseas now, for years")*

"And your people, they still have an interest in her?"

"Yuh mad? From 'im bruk up, all now shi nuh look 'pon 'im." *(Are you mad? From he was beat up, she has not even looked on him.)*

Whether it was the rum, being tired and just wanting to get back to my bed or stupid recklessness, or a mixture of all three, I began:

"Are you guys for real? I never heard such foolishness in my life. Are you really telling me that the two of you have been, maiming and killing one another all these years over a piece of dried up old pussy that nobody even wants anymore???"

Total silence and like in the cartoons, for a good five seconds, you could hear only the crickets chirping and distant music. Again, I could see daddy, hands on head, "Jaysus, Mary and Joseph!!"

Their response came in unison:

"Miss Myra!!!! Yuh cyaan say dem tings!!!!" *(Miss Myra!!! You can't say things like that!!!)*

"I just did. I suggest you guys think about that before you fire another shot, throw another bottle bomb, pick up a knife or otherwise look to settle this with violence. The reality is you could hardly even remember what started this, it's time to stop the foolishness and put an end to it all. Now, can I please go back home to my bed?"

I blamed the rum and tiredness for the unsteadiness as I rose. Better to be thought an alcohol lightweight than, for them to realise that fear of their reaction shook me to the core as it dawned on me what I had just said and to whom.

They were still laughing as I got in the car, slapping one another on the back:

"Piece a dried up ould pussy hahaha hahaha hahaha – Lawd shi don't easy, dried up ould pussy cho!!!! Pass di 'Special' nuh?" *(Piece of dried up old pussy, cho!!!! Pass the 'Special, no?)*

My head was pounding and my stomach churning, I could feel another weight loss moment coming on.

Some days later I was in the office at the Centre and heard a commotion at the gate so I went up to investigate.

On either side of the gates was a crowd, shouting and screeching at one another. I managed to get a level of quiet and discovered yet another cuss-cuss over a man, the usual. Both girls were shouting over one another to give me their side of the story, though, in truth, I don't think I heard a word through the volume.

Both sides of the crowd began chipping in again with threats flying in both directions and some bending down to pick up stones off the roadside. Again, I drew up my five feet four and, in my best 'British Nanny' tone, yelled:

"PUT THOSE DOWN!!!!!"

As I finished the word 'down', a rock thrown from the back of the crowd to my right landed squarely on my left foot. A communal sharp intake of breath, everyone froze silently, like 'Simon Says', then a bellow:

"Is who lick Miss Myra??" *(Who hit Miss Myra??)*

Seeing foot soldiers on both sides moving quickly away, I realised they were going for guns and this was about to escalate. Knowing this could end fatally for someone if I didn't do something to deflate the situation, with all the indignation I could muster I yelled:

"Lick who my youth? Did you hear me yelp or cry out? Did I tell you someone lick me?"

With that I turned and walked back down the churchyard

as best I could, given the pain level, trying desperately not to wince or limp.

I don't believe for one moment that I gave a particularly convincing performance, but the gesture was accepted as hoped, a signal to stop hostilities, at least for the day. In the office, I pulled out the First Aid Kit and cleaned and dressed the graze on the top of my foot which now began to bleed profusely.

Sipping gently at a rum and Coke over loads of ice from my coffee mug, it crossed my mind that maybe ducking bullets is not all about getting low, sometimes we have to bite our lip and pretend it doesn't hurt, for the sake of peace.

Sometimes we have to ignore our own pain in order to prevent the pain of others and besides, the foot wasn't broken, it healed quickly and well, so no real harm was done. In fact, I was told my respect levels in the community had just risen considerably.

Yes, it did dawn on me that I didn't have to be here taking these risks. I could go home and just visit the north coast in the winter months, but for whatever reason, I had to keep coming back. The very things that were driving me away, were calling me back. The pain and suffering of the children and elders, the inter and intra community violence were overwhelming and I wanted to stay far away from it. Yet my heart and spirit said come back, do what you can, care for an elder, nurture a child, hug a bad-man.

KINGS HOUSE

Whenever I was in London I always went to see my friend Delores Cooper at the Jamaican High Commission, either to have a coffee or lunch whereby I would update her on what was happening on the projects and in the various communities I was involved with in Jamaica.

Additionally, I would attend whatever functions the Jamaican High Commission put on during my stay. One such function, was a visit from Sir Howard Cooke, (then) Governor General of Jamaica. A lovely, jolly man with a keen sense of humour, who talked about his teaching days in Portland and Montego Bay.

I was introduced to him after his talk and over a rum cream he decided I wasn't really Irish, but must surely come from St. Elizabeth where there is a large contingent of German descendants, very light skinned and white. He gave me his card and invited me to come visit him at King's House when I got back to Jamaica, I should just call and make an appointment. I accepted his invitation and accordingly arranged a visit.

On the appointed day, I chartered a taxi from Three Miles and arrived as directed at nine-forty five a.m. to meet with the protocol officer beforehand. I was led into the amazing hallway, with its magnificent stairway. The protocol officer came and explained the procedure to me stating that I would be taken in and announced, I would spend ten to twenty minutes with His

Excellency and unfortunately, the house photographer was out sick so no photographs could be taken.

At 10.00 a.m. I was led into the reception room and announced. Sir Howard got up and greeted me, a short handshake followed by a hug,

"Ah my Irish friend from St. Elizabeth"

We sat and talked for about twenty or so minutes when the protocol officer returned, knocked gently and opened the door.

"Your Excellency?"

"Ah good man, right time, bring two coffees please, I don't have any more visitors due for now do I?"

"No your Excellency."

So for the next hour and a half, Sir Howard and I chatted about everything from cricket (seemed to be his favourite), music, theatre to politics and the 1980 election war and its continued repercussions on the (now) garrison communities. In that time, we enjoyed two more coffees, the second with little pastries.

I found Sir Howard to be a very forthright man, knowledgeable in many areas and unafraid to discuss the not-so-nice side of Jamaica in very real terms.

As I was leaving, Sir Howard gave me a signed copy of his biography titled, They Call Me Teacher.

GENEROSITY

I have come to understand that I have the most amazing family, who are very supportive in every way. Much of my travel up to 2003 had been made possible with savings and gifts from family and friends. Several sponsors came on board buying tickets, video camera (and tapes), over the counter medications, books and all sorts.

It was time to formalize the charitable status of the work that was now evolving in Jamaica. My brother Mickey, sister Maggie and friend Valerie formed a board and The Griffin Charitable Trust was born. We named the trust in honour of Daddy who more than once described himself to me as 'a penniless philanthropist'. We received our registration and number from the Charities Commission as I prepared to return to Kingston to get ready for summer school.

My ex-husband's uncle (Lincoln "Len" Dyke), was a pioneer in black business in the U.K. His wife came from Tower Hill, Jamaica and they had lived on Lothian Avenue off Olympic Way before migrating to London. Uncle Dyke, as my children called him, was an entrepreneur, an activist, a keen Garvey-ite (follower of Marcus Garvey philosophies) and always ready to help anyone in some form or other.

During my U.K. stays, I would always stop off in Palmers Green and update Uncle Dyke on what I had been doing in Jamaica. He seemed particularly happy that I had "chosen" Tower

Hill, although very concerned about the politics and more so about the violence. Uncle's wife had come from Tower Hill, they lived on Lothian Avenue before migrating to the UK and her mother (Miss Dada) lived at 48 Tamarind Turn, until her passing in the late 1980's. On this trip, Uncle asked if he could help me by supplying some 'school' resources which his friend Mr. Forbes could ship for us. Happy to accept his kind offer I went to meet Uncle at the wholesalers at Crouch End as arranged for 12 noon. Mr. Singh the proprietor, gave me a message from Uncle which stated I should go ahead and start selecting what I wanted. By 1.00 p.m. there was still no sign of Uncle, so I phoned him, only to find that he hadn't left home yet. I asked if we should do this another day,

"No, no my dear, you go on and shop 'til I reach"

"OK, what's my budget?"

"Oh my dear, just make yourself happy"

"How happy am I allowed to get??"

"How happy do you want to be?? Make yourself as happy as you like"

Really? No budget restriction.... That's dangerous, especially in my hands, worse I can spend it on the children in Jamaica!

Mr. Singh and I went through every shelf and box in the place, putting aside six each of every reading and story book, six each of every craft set, boxes of water paints of every hue, brushes, exercise books, sketch pads, pencils, colour pencils, wax crayons, colour craft papers, junior cricket sets and balls of every size and possible usage.

Uncle Dyke arrived as the last of the goods were going along the conveyor to the cashier and enquired how much the bill was. Looking at the till screen we had gone over the three thousand pounds mark, moving towards four. I wondered if maybe I had gone a little too far, but he just pulled out his chequebook, got Mr. Singh to throw in some 'brawta' (free extras) and arranged immediate delivery to Mr. Forbes. We then headed off for a late lunch. We discussed at length how and to whom the goods would be distributed when they arrived and how much should be kept for the programmes of the newly formed Griffin Trust.

We headed off to Forbes shipping off Tottenham High Road and assisted in the packing of all our goodies into a huge piano crate addressed to me at St Paul's Churchyard, Kingston.

The crate arrived in Kingston some weeks later and was received by Porter Brothers who cleared the goods, kept them until I could organise their distribution and gave us huge discounts by waiving their own fees and storage costs.

The crate was opened at St. Paul's with much joy and anticipation. All items were designated to various schools and preparations for the handing over ceremonies got underway. We do love a fanfare and reason to celebrate in Jamaica. My wonderful artiste friends made it their business to cover all five schools. Luciano, Mikey General, Lukie D, Singing Melody and Dean Fraser all turned out as requested.

Thanks to the amazing generosity of Lincoln (Len) Dyke, over a thousand children at Seaward Primary and Junior High (Olympic Way), Trinitarian Basic (Cockburn Pen), St Paul's Basic (Tower Hill), St Patrick's Primary (Waterhouse) and Little Angels Basic (White Wing) benefitted directly from his gift. Each school received reading corners containing over one hundred reading and story books, a junior cricket set, two footballs, two netballs, craft corners equipped with paints, brushes, craft paper, crayons, sketch pads, scissors and other arts and crafts materials. The after-school programme was equally well equipped and there was still tons of toys and goodies to use as progress incentives for the after-school and summer school attendees.

The Association of Jamaicans (North London) was another early sponsor who also helped us to create a reading centre at St Paul's, by shipping ten barrels of books of all genres and reading abilities across all subjects with a significant number on black history and the Caribbean.

Mr. Palmer at Jetstar Records in North West London, was (while the company was still running) a most loyal and consistent sponsor from day one, providing me with most of my travel assistance, emergency funds when unexpected medical expenses came up and a host of other help and support.

Air Jamaica gave me extra bag allowance and discounted fares. I even got bumped up to First Class on occasion and was always offered the opportunity to stand down if the flight was overbooked (giving me a cash compensation payment, an all expenses night at a good hotel in the U.K. or the U.S.A. and first-class cabin for flight/s) and I only ever arrived a day late.

COMING TOGETHER

The second Friday of May 2003 I got a last-minute invitation to bring elders to a 'Health Fair' the following day. We had a significant number of housebound elders who rarely got out to the clinic so I focused on those, arranging for taxis to meet me at certain points across the communities to ferry folk to St. Mary's on Molynes Road.

I had just come out of William Crescent and was heading towards Calladium and Tamarind Turn when I heard two men arguing behind me, it was obvious that they were considerably the worse for a few too many drinks (at-approximately 9.30 a.m.). I looked behind and given that they appeared to be in their late fifties, I thought no more about it, although they were both threatening to go for 'dem strap (gun) and 'lass' (machete). I stopped by Tamarind Turn, got one of my elders, known as Noisy ready and had two of the youth carry him in his chair to the corner of Tower Avenue to wait for the taxi.

As I turned down onto Tower Avenue heading towards Calladium Crescent, there was a piece of cussing and tracing coming from a man to the left. I'm really not sure how I missed the pistol in his hand, but I never noticed it. I turned and carried on, then I saw his opponent coming out of his yard with a machete in one hand and a deadly looking ratchet knife in the other. I moved considerably faster towards my destination, then boom, boom, boom the third of which was followed by "ppffftt" and a stream of hot air, as it passed me, very close, way too close for comfort. I grabbed my skirt and ran as fast as my legs could carry me down the Avenue and round onto Calladium, ducking into the side of the corner building. This same niche was occupied by several children from the Crescent, rolling around and laughing, almost in unison:

"Miss Myra, wi neva kno seh is so yuh could a run – Merlene Ottey don't 'ave nutten 'pon yuh jus' now". *(Ms Myra, we never knew you could run like that, Merlene Ottey has nothing on you just now).*

Whilst I joined in their merriment, my mind was on Noisy on the corner, the other elders waiting to be picked up and finding a way to get the gunplay off the street, at least during the day.

By now, I had trained four ladies from across the communities who were providing home care services to twelve elders in need. They went out in pairs, bathed the elders, took blood pressure readings (we had some nice electronic equipment donated) changed and laundered their bedding and clothes. The safety of my team was paramount and the needs of the elders critical so we had to get some kind of ceasefire in the area.

With the help of Bibi and Mother Smith, a respected matriarch from Tower Hill, I was able to arrange a meeting with the 'matriarchs' which led to our sitting with all the major corner leaders at first one on one, then gradually increasing until we got to the point where we had thirty-four corner leaders and community dons together in the one room. One of the local businessmen allowed us to use his club which was on the third floor of the local plaza, there was only one stairway up and down which, it crossed my mind, might be in contravention of fire regulations.

We had called the meeting for two p.m. in the certain knowledge that none of the men would appear before two-thirty p.m. As two-thirty struck they filtered in and settled themselves in the seats around the meeting table (two sheets of four feet by eight feet ply across the pool table,) nicely covered in a piece of red material. In the middle on one side sat two senior local JCF officers, there at the invitation of the 'leaders". At 3.00 p.m. we were ready to get down to business.

First order of the day, prayer followed by taking the issues one by one. There had been a number of drive-by shootings and early morning raids over the past couple of months and barricades were the order of the day on many roads, particularly at night time, some twenty-four hours and often manned. The police were insisting that all barriers be removed. Whilst in principle we agreed, the reality was that some people were not at the table and they were the most active in the drive-by shootings.

Various subjects were discussed, and occasionally it got quite heated with men almost chest to chest across the table, at which point I would slap the table hard and in my best 'strict British nanny voice' say

"Now, now gentlemen, please, this is not how we behave at meetings"

Inside I was praying:

"Thank you, Lord, please don't let them get too het up or be armed, Amen."

Outside a barrage of gunshot went off and all I could think was that we had been set up and were all about to be killed. A couple of the foot-soldiers went downstairs and came back, spoke to their leaders and it was decided that the gunfire had nothing to do with us. The meeting continued with the fervent (silent) thanks to God that they hadn't been armed.

Eventually, a general consensus was reached with the leaders and the police that while the majority of barricades would go, Grassquit Lane and Cling Cling would remain for the time being and that daylight retaliations would cease. Meeting over we all got ready to leave and as I bade each man goodbye, we hugged, as we hugged, I realised that in fact, almost all were armed.

The daylight ceasefire was working well until about three days before I was due to fly home. Early morning around seven-thirty on my way out to Olympic Way, we heard the sound of a gunshot with that sickening thump you hear when the bullet hits flesh, it sounded like it came from over Grassquit Lane, just across the road. When I went across I found out that the victim was little Davonte Lawler, three years old, bright as a button, sharp as a nail, confident, cheeky and so much more. He had a smile as wide as the Nile and could be seen regularly marching behind his grandfather in a perfect imitation of him, the bad man style dip and stride, dip and stride.

"Granddad, yuh can buy mi a h'ice-cream?" *(Grandad, can you buy me an ice cream?)*

I couldn't fathom how this could have happened, where was the barricade? we knew this was possible, that's why it was agreed the barricade would stay, how could they, a baby? Apparently just ten minutes before the drive-by, police removed the barricade from the road and the perpetrators freely drove through, not aiming for Devonte, but bullets have no eyes.

Horrifying as the death of a three-year-old is, this three-year-old came from a large family of leaders spread over several turfs, the implications of Devonte's death were potentially, even more horrifying.

I tried without luck to get everyone together again before I left for London. I just hoped I could link with some of the 'bigger heads', now in the U.K., to try settle things down somehow, at least by day.

MURPHY'S LAW

Just so you know, every time I flew out of Kingston on Air Jamaica, I expected to get either a bag check or a body search, sometimes both! The assumption always, that I was transporting drugs. Who knows, maybe it was the dreadlocks, maybe the frequency of travel or maybe even my Kingston 11 address. Whatever their reasoning, I always liked to be prepared for these eventualities.

June 10 2003, with a long day behind me and a nighttime flight ahead I decided to take my bags with me when I was leaving the house and stored them in the office at the centre until it was time to head for the airport.

As the car pulled up at the departure terminal, we could see a number of white men working alongside the Jamaican customs officers, and I began searching for the luggage keys. No luck! We did another circuit of the airport roadway, stopped at the gas station and purchased new locks, as I knew they would be a necessity.

Stepping through the door I asked the security officer if she had something to pop the locks on my bags as I knew for certain that my bags would be checked and I couldn't find the keys. She said she didn't have anything but that if they wanted to open my bags, the customs guys had the means to do so.

I joined the queue for the Air Jamaica flight and was approached by two British Officers. One was very tall and slim, obviously a police officer and the other was much shorter and a little rounder. I didn't think he was tall enough for police so I assumed immigration or customs.

"Excuse me, madam, can I ask where you are travelling today"

"London"

Holding out their IDs to me, they asked for my passport and introduced themselves,

"Andrew T, Her Majesty's Customs and Excise and Chris Hobbs, London Metropolitan Police. Would you mind identifying your bags and follow us please."

This I did and they carried the two suitcases to a search-table where we were joined by a tall JCF officer named Jack.

"Can I ask where you have been staying"

"Keys please"

"Phillipo Avenue, Kingston 11, sorry I couldn't find them getting out of the car"

There was an exchange of knowing glances between the three of them that said, "We have tonight's courier".

"That's okay Miss, we can open it"

"Fine with me, can you put these new locks on when you're done"

"So Miss, How long have you been in Jamaica this time? I see you travel frequently, what do you do?"

"Six weeks. I volunteer in the communities working with children and elders"

"Where?"

"Olympic Gardens"

"What? Kingston 11 Olympic Gardens? Doing what?"

"We have set up an after-school and elder's home-care programme and we're just getting ready for our second Summer Camp, bringing the children together from across the communities"

They then began the examination of my laptop.

"It doesn't switch on"

"No, the battery doesn't work anymore"

"We are going to have to take this and check it out". They were confident I was hiding something.

Everything was x-rayed, searched thoroughly and swabbed for traces of illicit drugs before I was given the all clear to proceed.

As I was leaving them I bumped into one of the Narcotics officers I knew from around the community. His grand-aunt was in our elders' care programme. We greeted one another as always with a hug and cracked a joke or two exchanging notes on 'Auntie's' latest escapade. One more hug and I headed off to the departure lounge and could hear the British officers ask him how he knew me.

Sometime later in the departure lounge I saw the two British Officers come through looking around red faced and frantic, people noticed and curiosity getting the better of them began watching them to see what was up.

Panic!!! I knew I had done nothing wrong, but still, alarm bells rang in my head, the lost keys, the cases and laptop in the Centre from six that morning, over eight hours!! I knew some very unsavoury and dodgy characters and I knew what they were capable of. I also knew it wasn't above them to have added something to the luggage while it was at the Centre. Surely not? Yes possible, but surely not probable, who would do that to me?? Greater panic as Andy and Chris spot me and move directly, hurriedly toward me, all eyes following.

"Ms Myra, can we call you that?"

"Yes, can I help you?"

Handing me their business cards, they began speaking in perfect timing, one behind the other.

"We have just been talking to our Jamaican colleague"

"He told us all about what you are doing. Tower Hill's a pretty rough place. We've driven through Seaward Drive and Olympic Way, it's rough!"

"Thank you for being so nice about the search"

"No problem, I'm used to it, it's a regular occurrence"

"We have our job to do, and you do kind of fit the profile. Again, we're sorry"

"Yes. In our job, we have lifted couriers who had left their children behind. We took a drive through the areas some of them came from. We started a Charity to help some of these children stay in school. "

"Last year we raised some money which was distributed by the British High Commission, but it went to children in uptown schools. We want to reach the children in the inner city"

"Oh, no worries about that. Inner city children often go to uptown schools, given the opportunity," I said. "For some children, the problem is the cost of the annual fee, books, or a pair of shoes, or a uniform, fares or lunch money"

"When are you back in Jamaica?"

"Three weeks"

"We'll be back in the U.K. by then. Can we link before you return to Kingston?"

These two guys, Chris and Andy (as we have come to know them) would soon become our guardian angels.

Three weeks later after leaving the Air Jamaica check-in desk at Heathrow, I met with Chris and Andy. We chatted over coffee, I gave them a video we shot of the Summer Camp closing ceremony and copies of the Newsletters I had produced documenting the progress. We agreed to keep in touch and they said they would be sending me the proceeds of their upcoming Disco, to assist with back to school expenses. I spent the next eight weeks, running Unity Summer Camp 2003.

While Summer Camp was in session things were quiet across the communities, during the day, but evenings and nights could be a very different story. Gunshots would ring out almost every night, near or not so near. Though I was not as expert as the children at identifying the individual weapons, it wasn't long before I learned to recognise that thump sound made when bullet connects with flesh.

One evening I was sitting in the front yard of Phillipo Avenue, perched on a couple of blocks, feet soaking in a pan of icy cold water. I had been on my feet almost all day, meeting children who would fit the criteria for back-to-school help. I was playing a clapping game with two toddlers who were amusing me and had just placed my phone in my lap. Suddenly a barrage of gunshots rang out from along Henry Morgan Road, splintering the corner of the house and I heard that ominous thump sound of the bullet hitting flesh nearby. I jumped up, grabbed the toddlers and ran for the house.

When we emerged sometime later, Jermaine seventeen years old, his mother's only child, a tall, slim, quiet, scholarly boy, studying for his CAPE exams, lay dead at the side of the gate. Three JCF officers were standing over him muttering "Ah nuh im yuh know". (*"That's not him you know"*) I felt every beat of his mother's broken heart as I held her and that gut wrenching, deep burning feeling in my 'belly bottom' like it is being torn out, a youth I knew and loved. What I felt couldn't match his mother's pain.

Again, I was faced with the brutality that is meted out to young men in the inner cities by agents of the State, without fear of accountability. I learned that evening, when police say a man or youth shot after them, it was not necessarily at that time, it could have been months, even years before. The 'suspect' for whom Jermaine was mistaken, was considerably older, at least twice his girth, distinctly shorter and had a run-in with those same officers some weeks before. It is very easy, apparently, to mistake a tall, slim youth for a short-ish, rotund man because they're both wearing their hair in cornrows and wearing similar red shirts, weeks after an incident.

When I got back to the yard my phone sat staring at me from the bottom of the pan of water. Those were the days when your number went with the handset. Panic, I don't have Chris' number anymore and he no longer has mine.

Over the next four days, Mark and I walked the length and breadth of Olympic Way from Three Mile down to Seward Drive, visiting families and talking to schools until we had a list of some fifty children and their specific needs. Myself, Mark and Nicky began the difficult task of selecting who would be our first awardees targeting first those who had just passed GSAT and were heading for High School. A number on the list, both boys and girls had passed for the 'traditional' high schools, namely Merle Grove, Immaculate, Queens, Jamaica College, Kingston College, St. Georges, Calabar etc., while the balance either remained in their Primary / All-Age (to Grade 9) or were placed in various secondary/high schools in Kingston.

We needed to get the balance right, not just help the children doing really well, but help those who would otherwise be overlooked. We selected a total of twenty-seven (twenty-five moving to secondary level and two into vocational training).

The list completed I now needed to contact Chris. I knew Chris was a Trident officer, but also knew that he was rarely stationed in any particular office. I had to track him down and give him the U.K. office address in order for him to send that much-needed cheque.

With my new phone in hand I tried desperately to remember his phone number but wasn't having much luck. I tried ringing the MET headquarters and dialling random extensions, after several attempts and what was maybe the fifth time I dialled another random extension and Chris answered the phone!! He just answered the phone at someone else's desk. Joyful at reconnecting, we exchanged numbers again and the necessary details for the cheque. I let him know that after exhaustive walking, talking and visiting of schools we had finally selected twenty-seven worthwhile awardees.

It was now time to prepare for back to school. Jamaica being Jamaica, all the schools have different banks and different book lists, even for the same grade. This entails going to various suppliers for books and different bank branches in order to pay fees. Many days were spent in long incredibly slow bank queues (because there were no means to pay across banks), fighting our way in and out of book stores, negotiating discounts, finding the correct uniform materials and shoe sizes. Eventually, all twenty-seven children were kitted out ready for 'September Morning', with the required fees paid to enable them to begin the academic year.

In November 2003, Chris and Andy were once again back in Kingston on duty and I thought it would be nice for them to meet all the children they had helped.

We met at Olympic Gardens Police Station, where accompanied by Jack, (from the airport stop) and Mark we began a journey that touched them deeply. We spent time in Tower Hill meeting awardees Tijani, Sasha, Pebbles, Kimberly, Josh, Dwight and so on through the communities arriving at the bottom end of West Bay Farm Road just before dusk. We stood, sipping cool Red Stripe beers waiting for Miss Del who, with neither chick nor child of her own, had taken in a number of children from the community, one of them named Andrew was an awardee. The guys wanted to meet and thank her for supporting Andrew. Miss Del arrived as darkness began to draw. There are no street lights along the lane just the odd 40-watt bulb hanging on a gate post or a tree limb. Knowing that the inner city is a very different place after dark, and two white men and a white lady leaning up against an SUV could become targets, Miss Del and I suggested it might be time to leave.

Andy, who was very sure of himself, said

"Oh we'll be okay, we've been to Waterhouse before you know."

Jack leaned over and in a stage whisper replied

"Errmm Andy, please note that back then, we were in a bullet-proof vehicle, armed and it was broad daylight. We have none of those advantages right now, so I agree with Miss Myra, time to go."

Since the summer of 2003, Chris and Andy have continued to support our children in education in Jamaica to the tune of over twenty thousand pounds over the years. They are my back-to-school angels.

A number of the children assisted have done well, one is now President of the Commonwealth Youth Council, one an aspiring politician, several University graduates, nurses, bank workers, both in Jamaica and overseas.

SUMMER CAMP

The registration queue for Unity Summer Camp 2003 stretched almost the full two hundred feet to the church gate. Children lined up excitedly, some were accompanied by adults, many were not.

Whilst there was tension across the community because two recent deportees looked to regain lost turf, it was pretty much quiet during the day, but could be explosive at night.

Summer Camp 2003 saw an amazing change in that with the permission of their "bigger heads", some of the foot soldiers were trained to assist the Band members with sports, play and reading activities for the children.

On the second Friday of Camp, I watched a couple of the foot-soldiers swinging the little ones on the old tyre swing, hanging from the Tamarind tree behind the centre. Blacks, a solemn looking youth seventeen, maybe eighteen, long thin and as his nickname suggests, very dark skinned, sat on the 'story rock' staring up at the sky thoughtfully.

"Ms Myra yuh know seh mi neva did know mi madda?" *(Miss Myra, yuh know that I have never known my mother?)*

"Sorry about that honey, she died?"

"Nuh, she jus' lef mi pon mi Granny bed t'ree weeks old, yuh know; T'ree weeks, yuh believe dat?? All now she nuh look 'pon mi, an a have nerve fi sen message fi seh she an mi likkle bredda dem a'right a farrin, nuh even sen a sweetie." *(No, she just left me on my Granny's bed at three weeks old, you know. Three weeks old, can you believe that?? Up to this day, she hasn't even looked on me and has the nerve to send message to say she and my little brothers are alright overseas, not even sent a sweetie!!!)*

"Yuh know seh is jus yuh an di dods heva mek mi feel like s'maddy?? Mi Granny neva like not a bone inna mi body. Jah know." *(You know that it's just you and the Don ever make me feel like somebody?? My Granny never liked a bone in my body. God knows)*

"Sorry to hear that, my youth. So, what are your plans for the future, you have any?"

"Yes Miss, mi 'ave plans, mi 'ave dreams. Mi wan' fi be a h'architect. Mi can draw good an mi can measure almos wid mi y'cye. Mi nuh so good pon di book learning, but mi love fi draw an mi good pon di maths." *(Yes Miss, I have plans, I have dreams. I want to be an architect. I can draw well and I can measure with just my eye, almost. I'm not so good on the written work, but I love to draw and I'm good with maths)*

"Mi wan go a classes fi get mi English an Physics so mi can learn fi be one h'architect. If mi can teach di likkle pickney a Camp, mi mus' can learn dem tings, don't??"*(I want to go to classes to get English and Physics so I can learn to be an architect. If I can teach the little kids in Camp, I must be able to learn those things, don't you think??)*

"Absolutely, my youth. It's up to you. My dad always used to say 'You don't fail until you give up'. So if you don't pass your exams the first time, just study some more and try again."

Looking around him, he sighed deeply got up and left the churchyard with a solemn "Laters".

Saturday morning, Nicky was at the gate with the news that Blacks had been killed in crossfire on Back Road the previous night. I was heartbroken and not a little shook up. All that kept going through my head was our conversation, playing like a musical loop, over and over again. "Mi wan fi go a class fi be one h'architect." *(I want to go to class to be an architect).* I still see his face, that dual look so common in the inner city, one of hope and yet total despair at the same time.

I prepared some worksheets for what I thought was much-needed grief counselling with the Campers on Monday. Though I hope I didn't show it, I was totally floored by the cool, calm, this is part of our daily lives, "a nuh nutten *("it's nothing")* manner that came across in the sessions. Only the younger ones seemed to be phased by the loss of 'one of our own'. I realised then, it is always 'one of our own' for them, family, friend, schoolmate or acquaintance, it's always one of their own. I think that was when I realised that the eyes of the younger ones held a different light to that of the older ones, say, from seven or eight up.

Camp continued with the classes each preparing an item for Blacks' funeral and a segment for the Camp Closing Ceremony.

We took the children to Tinson Pen Aerodrome to experience the planes. Had a day trip to Hellshire Beach and planned to go to Ital Spring again on the last day, the day after the Ceremony.

Once again we were blessed with all the necessities for our Camp Closing Ceremony which were either donated or hugely discounted backpacks, stationery, khakis, the works.

This time the lovely Warrior King (a very talented Jamaica reggae artiste) came along and edutained all those present with uplifting lyrics, historical fact and encouraging words to young and old alike.

Our Friday trip to Ital Spring got off to a late start. Chartering the route buses as we normally did was proving difficult to arrange, it being the week before 'September Morning' and the route was very busy. Eventually, we headed off around 11.00 a.m. with the warning that we may be back late. Reasons given were that the route was busy and the buses won't be able to come back until the shops are shut in Town.

We had a fabulously relaxing and enjoyable day, everyone filling up once again on sprats, festival and bag juice and also splashing and playing in the clear waters of the spring.

The buses didn't reach us until almost 6.00 p.m. as dusk was closing in. By the time we got back to Tower Avenue it was after 7.00 p.m. and dark. I noticed a crowd around the churchyard gates and surmised it was the families concerned because we were so late. As we drew up to the gates a police jeep reversed out of the lane with its big search light beam focused on a body lying on the ground. It was Parroman.

Parroman 'looked after' St Paul's Lane and Ebony Road, whatever his position in things, I knew him as a well-read, humble Rasta. He was ever quick with jokes, deep in his reasonings and always looked for the peaceful solution to things. He was prepared to put himself on the line to facilitate peace. Everybody loved him, I never saw fear in the eyes of any person, man, woman or child who came into contact with him. I saw only respect and, in enough eyes, love.

I was a bit slow to react and the children started getting off the bus. Five-year-old Chrissie ran to her mother in the lane. "Smiler" I used to call her because she had this amazing smile that lit up not just her eyes, but her whole face and the entire room. Her eyes always sparkled giving the impression that she was constantly smiling.

Chrissie stood behind her mother peeping around her long skirt. She looked up at her mum who nodded to say 'he's gone'. She looked down at Parroman and looked up at me, her eyes wide. She looked down again and up at me once more and it was as if someone had flicked off a switch. The light of hope that kept her spirit so high, was gone, just like that, to be replaced by a sadness that has never left her eyes.

To this day, I am haunted by the pain and anguish that I witnessed in Chrissie's eyes that night.

I debated long and hard about coming back to Jamaica. When the very words I had spoken to Blacks came back to me "My dad always used to say 'You don't fail until you give up'..." and I knew that if I didn't come back there was no chance to reignite the light and I had to try.

SHOE BOXES

C hris and Andy were both deeply affected by what they saw during their community walkabout in Kingston and when they returned to the U.K. they immediately launched a shoe box appeal among their, friends, families and colleagues. They enlisted the help of the Foreign and Commonwealth Office towards the shipping to the British High Commission in Kingston and distribution of the shoe boxes to the children in the communities in time for Christmas. Consequently, they opened the doors of the British High Commission to me on both a social and professional level.

The lovely Linda Lane (whose husband Paul led the community projects small grants section), came to visit and fell in love with the community. Linda invested significant amounts of her time, energy and personal finance engaging other members of the diplomatic corps at the British and Canadian High Commissions and the US Embassy.

The shoe boxes arrived at the High Commission and were brought to the centre by a cadre of ladies including Linda, a couple each of DfID (Department for International Development) and British Council staff.

The ladies and I took a walk into the community and left the driver and escorts to move the goodies from the truck to the basic school and watch over them until we got back.

When we got to Calladium Crescent we were greeted with

shouts of "Teacher, teacher!!!" from Greg as he ran lopsidedly up the road, arms outstretched. Greg was fifteen and had Cerebral Palsy which resulted in an unsteady gait, speech and learning difficulties and severe epilepsy. He was always very friendly and loving to everyone, even when teased and had decided that my name was 'teacher'.

Greg lived with his father and his father's foster mother Ma Mae, eighty-four years old who was short, round and sweet. Ma Mae was also responsible for two boys nine and eleven years old left by another foster child before heading to foreign three years previously. The house was very old and in pretty rough condition but they all managed and were supportive of one another and everyone watched out for Greg.

Linda fell in love with this family and for the remainder of her stay in Jamaica would regularly take the boys out and treat them uptown style.

When we returned to the centre all the boxes had been sorted into gender and age ready for the children who, having enjoyed fried chicken, chips, soda, cake and ice-cream, were now looking forward to their gifts. There was one box each for all the children who had attended Summer Camp, one for each of the children of those who had assisted and we still had forty boxes over which we took to the children at Mustard Seed (A non-profit organization dedicated to the residential care of children and adults with a range of developmental and physical disabilities). I have always believed in sharing the blessings, it is how I was raised.

The Foreign and Commonwealth Office and the British High Commission gave us grants to extend the Centre in March 2004 and funded our Home Care Service and Training programmes for the next year.

When I arrived back in Kingston I commenced arrangements to initiate the structural works. The proposed extension did not require planning permission, so it was a matter of finding a contractor who could follow the plans and remain within the budget, or so I thought.

As resources came in, it was then the intra-community politics became evident and started to play out. The only permissions we needed were from the newly re-formed Progressive League, but we were constantly being given the runaround. It got to the point where the corner leaders were preparing to 'remove' the obstacle. I did not want any more war in the community. I called a couple of the guys in London for advice on how to handle things, particularly the opposition that was revealing itself. I was advised I should go and see Mr. Coke in Tivoli and an introduction would be arranged.

I received a call on the Wednesday telling me to meet a gentleman in Coronation Market, to ask for a particular stall. I was already well known to a number of stall-holders as I regularly shopped there so I had no problem finding who I was looking for. Zion, a serious looking man with a menacing air about him, asked who had sent me and handed me his phone to call the number of the contact in the UK to verify my claim. After speaking to UK he made two calls and had one of his foot soldiers walk me over to Tivoli Square where I was introduced to Mr. Coke, otherwise known as Dudus.

We shook hands and he apologised saying that he couldn't stay to talk today but I should make an appointment with the gate-man for the following day.

Once again I was struck by how far my expectations were from the reality as I had expected a giant of a man. When using the nickname 'Short-man' in Jamaica, it could be used to describe someone very short or exceedingly tall, Dudus is definitely not tall. I have to be honest and speak as I find and as with many I have met, it is hard to reconcile the reputation with the man. He didn't seem in the least bit scary, was quite affable and humble really. I had expected to meet a giant of an ogre.

I returned to Coronation Market the next day, assuming I would follow the same routine. Zion told me I was good and should go on over to the square. My head whirled, I was so busy thinking about the whole rigmarole the previous day, I hadn't taken note of where we had turned left or right going into Tivoli. So, putting best foot forward, I stepped out and headed to what I hoped was the Square.

On every corner I was greeted with "Mawnin teacha" and just as I was feeling hopelessly lost, a young man decided he should escort me to the square. Once there I reported to the 'gateman' who directed me to go see the man in front of the centre, who would see me as Mr Coke was not available. So I went and spoke to the gentlemen, he appeared to be in his mid-thirties, early forties, tall, dark skinned and dressed in 'Sunday' pants and shirt with a hardback exercise book and pen in hand. He asked me several questions about me, about what I was doing in Jamaica, who I knew in London and how I knew them. I was then asked to come back the following day, then the next and the next. Each time I was 'interviewed' by a different man, same questions, different formats, the answers written in the same hardback exercise book. By the fifth visit, I was getting tired of repeating myself and running out of patience with all this rigmarole.

I'm not a red-head, but I am Irish and accordingly, I do have a temper, a bad one. One that will let the words fly from my lips before the brain has had a chance to filter them, one that will unknowingly (or uncaringly), speak thoughts aloud.

After wasting another hour answering the same questions, repeating the same answers, sitting on the bench outside the community centre, with a large, square jawed, light skinned, 'coolie', he then asked me one final one.

"So Miss, why you don't jus do wha di one man want, and jus lef the place?" In shock that a 'man' in the community wanted me to leave, albeit on political grounds, mixed heavily with Irish temper, I said,

"So what he's going feed my elders, send the pickney go to school?"

With that I snatched up my bag off the bench, looked him straight in the face, "You know what, the whole a unnu can kiss my wrinkly white arse!!!"

I spun on my foot and stomped briskly out towards, what I hoped would be, Spanish Town Road, to the sound of riotous laughter behind me. I half expected gunshot any moment.

I arrived on site at St Paul's next morning, to be greeted with one hundred concrete building blocks and an unsigned note:

"Gwaan do your ting, nuh watch nuh face." (*"Go ahead, do what you are doing, you don't need to worry"*)

I cannot say I know who sent them, but I know they meant the community good, opposition to the work ceased.

ELDERS TREAT

Happy that the children had their treats, we wanted to do something for the elders. Not just feed them but give them an exceptionally good time. While we were working across the communities, we had not yet managed to get the elders from the communities together in one place. So it transpired that we had ourselves an inter-community Christmas Treat bringing together over one hundred and twenty seniors from Three Miles to Bay Farm Road. We arranged the seating so that every table held at least one resident from each community.

We hired and set up trestle tables and chairs on the multipurpose court and borrowed a big tent from one of the other churches. We also brought in Macky and his sound system from over Cockburn Pen, with strict instructions to play pure oldies and Gospel.

The elders arrived, the youngsters ushered and seated them and served them food and drinks while they listened to the music. Mother Smith had made a huge pot of her infamous Rum Punch (very potent stuff) and a cup was served to all. The conversation flowed around the tables and there was much, "Lawd, mi nuh si yuh fi di longest" *(Lord, I haven't seen you in the longest time)*, "Is how much years? gal/man yuh still look good" *(How many years has it been? Girl/man, you're still looking good)* and even more exclamations of "'member when?" *(remember when?)*

As the music moved from Swing and Sam Cooke to Mento and then Ska and Rock Steady there was a movement among the elders. Chairs pushed back from the tables and there was a piece of leg shaking, foot turning and hip winding to show us all they still had it. Cake and ice cream demolished, followed by a gift for all, it was then time for the 'floor show'.

Thanks to Luciano, Mikey General, Milton Blake and other artistes, they had the most amazing up close and personal concert. For over an hour Luciano sang all of his classics, Sweep Over my Soul, It's Me Again Jah, Who's That Knocking? together with other classics from Bob Marley, Dennis Brown and Burning Spear. Then he started on the church gospel, There's a Flag Flying, When The Saints, Teach Me Lord and much more. The elders were elated and half the community gathered in and around the churchyard taking in the magical vibes.

After the party I escorted a pair of my elder ladies up to Top Tower, heading off the Avenue, they went to turn up Tamarind Turn.

"I thought you were both on the Avenue, why turn up here?"

"A nuh any and anybody can walk up di Avenue, Miss Myra" *(It's not everyone that can walk straight up the Avenue, Miss Myra)*

"What do you mean?"

"From di 'lection days, yuh cyaan jus walk certain place"*(From the time of the [1980] elections, you can't just walk through certain places)*

"Are you telling me, all these years you have to take a diversion half way round the community to reach your home on the Avenue?"

"Ah jus so di ting set, a Jamaica dis."*(That's just how it is, this is Jamaica)*

Smiling, but feeling angry I asked, "Ladies would you trust me to walk you along the Avenue to your houses, safely?"

Once again I see my father, hands on head, tearing at the little hair he had left, "Jaysus, Mary and Joseph!!!" Again a silent prayer:

"Father God, I know I keep putting you to the test like this. I know I keep taking chances with the life you have granted me. Keep us safe Lord. Let us reach our homes in one piece. Know Lord I would not step out into danger recklessly. Know too that your grace keeps me safe and gives me courage. I rely on your promises to Bless the Peacemaker. Amen."

"Whaa?? Miss Myra, yuh really woulda do dat???"*(What?? Miss Myra you'd really do that???)*

"Of course, come on."

We turned back onto the Avenue and headed up toward Top Tower. Along the way the two ladies chatted amiably:

"Is Ms Silva yaad dat?" *(Isn't that Ms Silvas house?)*

"Look like dem rich a farrin eeh!!!" *(Looks like they made money overseas!!!)*

"See Missa Chin deh?" *(Do you see Mr. Chin there?)*

"Missa Chin!! di bar look gud y'ear, Hail up Miss Chin f'mi!!"*(Mr. Chin!! The bar is looking good, you hear, say hello to Mrs. Chin for me!!)*

"'Member wen 'im did a look di two a wi???" *(Remember when he used to try date us both???)*

Peals of laughter came from them both.

"Dutty ould skettle, an 'im wife jus' up di road!!" *(Dirty old man, and his wife just up the road!!!)*

"Mi use fi tek 'im money an seh mi a guh meet 'im later. Later, which part??? Mi??" *(I used to take his money and say I would meet him later. Which part of later??? Me??)*

More laughter, we reach Top Tower.

"Goodnight ladies, sleep well."

"An yuh Miss Myra. Safe travels. Hail up di fambily, 'ave a Merry Christmas!!" *(And you Miss Myra, Safe travels. Say hello to your family, have a Merry Christmas!!)*

As I turned back down the Avenue they called out to me:

"Miss Myra, yuh know di bes part fi di hola day??" *(Miss Myra, do you know what was the best part of the whole day)*

I spun around smiling:

"No, tell me."

"A walking 'traight up di Avenue, long time wi nuh do dat." *(It was walking straight up the Avenue, it's been a long time since we did that)*

"Tanks an God Bless yuh, y'ear? walk good." *(Thank you and God bless you, you hear? Walk in safety)*

I must have looked like a fool as I walked back to St Paul's with a smile from ear to ear, chuckling along the way. I know my cheeks hurt by the time I got back.

I discovered that so deeply entrenched were enmities between turfs and families that there were various parts of the community which were only accessible to the residents of them by a long, convoluted walk or one along the edge of the gully-bank. Straight routes between A and B that I walked on a daily basis, were unavailable to those that lived there, even to the elders.

This was something we were able to change over time.

2004

PROGRESS

Whilst in London we received positive responses from several small U.K. grant givers including Rupert Cadbury at the Cadbury Trust, The Hilden Charitable Trust and London Kiwani's.

A small office was set up and manned voluntarily by myself, my nieces, Kelly and Hazel and later by an outside volunteer named Sophia.

These small grants enabled me to ensure that needy elders received vital medications and the feeding and care programmes were strengthened.

We also received notification of the success of our grant application to the British High Commission which allowed for us to extend the community centre, train and employ care workers for two years, equip the kitchen with a stove, a fridge and freezer and to purchase tables and chairs, plus basic office equipment.

I could hardly wait to return to Kingston and get started.

In those days, Air Jamaica had authorized extra bag allowance for my trips and I often met with Chris and/or Andy for a coffee (if they were on duty) before I flew out from Heathrow.

My New Testament friends at Wood Green, London had filled one of those huge market bags with goodies for the elders containing over the counter medications, heat rubs, string vests, cotton housecoats, pyjamas and toiletries. Mum had filled another bag with Beanie soft toys, teddy bears and treats for the children. Additionally, I had one bag which wasn't big but was heavy with paperwork and another with all the 'just a little sintings' *(just a little something)* I carried to Jamaica for family and friends.

Andy met me as I was about to check in. A lovely lady, French judging by the accent, started to weigh and check the bags, letting me know I was two bags in excess of the allowance. I asked her to check with the airline representative as an extra allowance had been granted. She made the call. While she was waiting for them to call her back Andy asked what was wrong. She told him that there was nothing noted on the manifest so she had to wait for a response from the representative.

They began to chat. Andy told her that he had been to Jamaica and had witnessed firsthand all the work that we do and explained all the projects we were involved in with limited resources. By the time he had finished, her cheeks were wet and her makeup beginning to run. She turned to me and said "Thank you" and proceeded to tag the bags and shove them along the conveyor, not waiting for the representative to call her back to OK it.

Over coffee, Andy and I discussed Summer School and he let me know that the charity he and Chris started (Airbridge Foundation) would like to bring some volunteer teachers from the U.K. to help us set up and run it. Amazing!! I was elated and so excited for the incredible wave of support and what it could achieve for the children.

MI DID A WARN YUH!

Nina was tall, slim and very, very dark. She lived in a one room shack off Olympic Way, her 'baby-father' had been shot by police in dubious circumstances, not to say he had been an angel, but the story of a police shoot-out, a man in bushes, chased into room.... wears thin when repeated so often, verbatim.

Even though Nina herself was now wanted by the police as her man was supposed to have a stash of cash and contraband, she remained at home or nearby, afraid that moving schools would cause more trauma to her 4-year-old daughter, who had just lost her dad.

The yard that backed onto my room in Mas Peter's house, was large and occupied by multiple families. Every morning and every evening the women of the yard would sit out by the gate on Henry Morgan Road and gossip. Unfortunately, Nina was the subject of much of that gossip and the brunt of their vicious 'tracing' as she passed daily to drop the little one to school and pick her up. The basic school was directly opposite the yard gate.

The yard 'matriarch' was Ms. Meg. A large, rotund, light skinned, once a pretty woman in her mid-forties, looking closer to sixty rather than fifty. She was a bitter, angry woman with a vicious tongue and I too had had a run in or two with her.

For a long time, myself and Nina just smiled at one another

when we passed and said 'good morning/afternoon', Nina's face always lit up and the little one echoed mummy's words with the same glowing smile.

One morning about a week after my return to Jamaica, Nina called to me as I crossed over Delisser on my way to Tower Avenue,

"G'morning, Miss Myra, yuh ave a time can talk wid mi likkle bit?" *("Good morning Miss Myra, do you have some time we can talk a little?")*

"Sure Nina, what's up?"

"Please mi a beg unnu, talk to di big ooman fi mi, mi a guh do dem sinting if'n dem nuh stop." *(Please, I'm begging you, talk to the women [in the yard with Meg]for me, I'm going to do something to them if they don't stop)*

"Come with me Nina, let's go talk away from here".

We took a bus to Three Miles and then another one to Town, sitting in William Grant Park on Parade, she opened her life to me.

I had always assumed her to be in her early to mid-twenties, but now found she had just turned nineteen, I realized then that she was only a child of fourteen when she became a mother.

She was a bright girl and had passed for Queens High School but was told by her mother that "if is der yuh wan guh, is bes' yuh start tek a man, cos mi nuh have dat der money." *(If that's where you want to go, you better take a man[to support you]because I don't have that kind of money).* Nina was only twelve years old at the time!

Of course, her pass had been the talk of the community, Queens was a good 'traditional' high school so the community was proud and loud about it and then the predators began to circle.

Growing up in the inner city, Nina knew that to survive she needed to align herself with a man who could protect her from the others, one who was feared and/or respected. She found one!

There had been no pressure from her 'sponsor' through Grade 7, the summer between Grades 7 and 8 he had taken her on various trips, again no pressure. Grade 8, he presented her as a 'gift' to six of his friends after he had taken her 'cherry' first, on Christmas morning after brunch.

She never went back to school. In the New Year, she was passed on to one of the bigger man's foot soldiers, who became her baby-father. They lived peaceably for the most part, though he had other women and girls, he 'protected' her from the 'others'.

When the police shot her baby-father they had come in search of guns and money, neither of which were found. Nina was left destitute after the burial expenses and homeless when she could no longer pay rent on the two roomed concrete house they had lived in. She subsequently moved into a ramshackle (though immaculately kept) board room with their daughter. Her father's death and then the loss of their home had deeply affected the little one who became withdrawn and developed a stammer. She was no longer the jolly girl skipping alongside her mother to and from school, full of chatter but, she and her mother always hailed me or returned my greeting with radiant smiles and a joyful wave.

Yes, I was aware that Nina was wanted by the police, but then so were the police officers that visited her regularly for sexual favours in return for their 'protection'. She never hid, she never changed the little one's school. She stayed in her yard, took care of her home and child, rarely venturing out other than the daily school walk.

After my conversation with Nina I stopped by Ms. Meg and asked that she and her crew keep the tracing (if they must trace at all), to Nina, leave her family and particularly her baby-father and child out of the argument. For a while, things quietened down somewhat.

About two weeks later, I remember it was a Wednesday morning, a little after seven-thirty when I heard them start on

Nina, calling her every dirty name they could think of, they heckled her as she approached the school gate. I ran out of the house and gate and as I approached the group I heard Nina growl,

"Please, mi dun beg unnu fi stop di fuckry, leave mi alone or mi a guh fine fi mi man gun and shoot yuh inna yuh bumba-hole!!!"*(Please, I've asked you already to stop the fuckery, leave me alone or I will go find my man's gun and shoot you in your backside!!!)*

With that Ms Meg railed back,

"Sooo unnu ave dead-lef gun an dead lef pickney, pity im neva dead lef yuh some a di money." *(So you have 'dead left'[inherited] gun, and 'dead left' child, pity he never left you some of the money)*

Nina glared at the group of laughing women, growling deeply,

"Member say, mi did a warn yuh!!!" *(Remember, I did warn you!!!)*

With that, she spun on her foot, put the little one through the school gate with a kiss and a hug and passed me for the first time ever without a greeting. I went inside and changed into street clothes and headed off to Nina's room which I found empty. I checked with Ms. Mitzy and Bredda to see if she had stopped by either of them to buy groceries, no one had seen her. I stood out on Olympic Way and waited for buses passing from Three Mile to Waterhouse, checking with conductors I knew whether she had taken a bus. I was told she had taken one to Three Mile and then boarded a Town bus. I could only wait for her to come back and hope she hadn't really gone for a gun.

I decided to remain at home so I would be around at 2.00 p.m. schools-out-time, when Nina usually collected her daughter. She arrived, went inside the school and miraculously ignored the tracing from across the road. I looked at the gossips and said

"One of these days, your vicious tongues will push her too far and I'm sorry for you when that day comes."

I crossed the road to Nina as she and the little one came out of school, we smiled, greeted and hugged one another.

"Mi sarry fi dis mawnin, mi neva mean fi pass yuh so" *(I'm sorry for this morning, I never meant to pass you like that [without greeting])*

"That's okay honey, but you had me worried, you don't usually go to Town on a Wednesday. You did so well ignoring them just now, proud a you girl"

"Fi dem time soon come, watch". *(Their time will soon come, watch)*

As I walked out onto the main road with them, Nina turned to me and gave me a big hug saying

"Miss Myra, mi jus wan fi say tanks fi wha yuh do fi mi and mi pickney an mi sarry fi any problem wha mi gi' yuh." *(Miss Myra, I just want to say thanks for what you've done for me and my daughter and I'm sorry if I gave you any problems)*

"Nina you never gave me a problem yet, I'm just glad if I have been able to help you. Though I don't see that I've done anything."

"Miss Myra, yuh dun lissen mi an yuh did hear wha mi did a say, yuh nah scorn me. Mi feel like a s'maddy roun yuh, thanks. Say bye-bye to Miss Myra baby-girl." *(Miss Myra, you listened to me, you heard what I said, with no judgement. I feel like somebody around you, thanks. Say bye-bye to Miss Myra, baby girl)*

I hugged them both goodbye and watched them as they walked up Olympic Way with a sad feeling that I would never see them again.

A little while later, I was in my room reading when I heard Nina yelling out on the road,

" Yo!!! dutty gyal Meg, seh wha unnu did a seh earlier, <u>seh</u> it, gwaan!!!" *(Hey, dirty girl Meg, say what you did earlier, say it, go on!!!)*

With that, I heard two shots, sounding like both bullets connected with their intended victim, which was followed by much screaming and shouting. When I got out into the street, there was no sign of Nina but what appeared to be the whole neighbourhood, crowded around the gate and there was Ms. Meg, who was screaming obscenities at all and sundry while holding onto her thigh which was bleeding profusely. She was scooped up by four burly men, deposited in the back of Mas James' truck and taken to KPH (Kingston Public Hospital), where she died some weeks later due to complications with diabetes.

That night they set fire to Nina's one room, but she had long vacated. I never heard from her again and still wonder to this day if she is still here in Jamaica or somewhere foreign??

STONE SOUP

Miss Fran, in her mid-eighties, painfully gaunt, hunched and always ready with a smile would dress up every Tuesday and head to the post office at Three Miles to collect mail from her 'family' overseas. She never had any children of her own, but in true Jamaican style, had taken in, nurtured and grown a number of other people's children over the years. Miss Fran lived in a one room board house, exceedingly dilapidated yet kept immaculately with red polished floor and steps that shone with the vigorous rubbing of the coconut brush she applied daily.

Though obviously in dire need of proper sustenance, she came to the centre regularly but never ate any meals there. She came for the social interaction and whatever medical assistance was provided as she had multiple chronic disorders including, arthritis, diabetes and 'pressure'.

Over time I got to know Miss Fran by listening to her amazing stories of the successes of her 'children' in foreign lands. From her, I learned the reality of "stone soup" and how Jamaican Pride can kill. She accepted dry goods from me to cook for herself (many Jamaicans, especially old time Jamaicans are very funny about who they eat food from) this at least ensured she had the basics.

I had arrived back from a London trip and popped in to Miss Fran with a special gift. A tantalizing aroma drifted over the zinc fence as I approached, something good was cooking. I stepped through the gate and called out for Miss Fran, she hollered back that she was in the outhouse at the rear of the yard, I settled down on the block at the side of the beautiful shining red step to wait for her. The smell coming from the pot sitting on the coal stove alongside me was making my mouth water and I could no longer resist taking a peek.

As I lifted the lid Miss Fran came around the side of the house letting out a startled shriek. I tried desperately to hide the shock I felt as I looked down into the clear water containing onion, scallion, garlic, thyme, literally three little spinners (small, sausage shaped boiled dumplings) and two small egg-shaped rocks, my introduction to 'stone soup'. I replaced the lid and assured her it smelled good and nutritious. I changed the subject by presenting her with a Rose scented soap and body lotion set sent over by one of my daughters, for one of my 'special' ladies. Miss Fran made much of the fact that the set came from Marks and Spencers, she had heard that the Queen shops there!

Suddenly she turned and hugged me tight and began sobbing, real heart wrenching, body-rocking sobbing. When she could speak again it poured from her

"Miss Myra, mi sarry, yuh know say is untruth mi tell yuh long time. Is only one a di pickney dem stay in touch, true, true." *(Miss Myra, I'm sorry, you know, for a long time I haven't told you the truth. It's only one of the children who stays in touch, honest, honest.)*

"Oh, sorry to hear that"

"Is 'im alone send a likkle change fi mi sometime. A nex one, a shi write pretty letter a Chrismus, but she nuh sen nutten an de others, is shi mek mi know ow dem is. But mi cyaan mek dem out deh know seh a so it guh. Mi mek dem believe say mi cris, di pickney wha mi grow a tek care a mi, mi ave nuff money an tings.... Yuh know ow much time mi gi weh food to a next s'maddy an a jus eat two cracker and drink a one bag juice?? Yuh know how much time mi a run likkle stone soup mek dem believe say mi a eat nuff, and mi siddung an a eat two so so dumpling, not even butter fi put pon dem?? Mi cyaan mek dem ave tings ova mi, dem a chat nuff already." *(It's he alone who sends a little money for me sometimes. Another one, she writes a pretty letter at Christmas, but she doesn't send anything else. As for the others, it's she who lets me know how they are. But I can't let those out there [in the community] know that's how it is. I make them believe that I'm fine, that the children I grew are taking care of me, I have enough money and things. Do you know how often I've given food to someone else and just eat two crackers and drink a bag juice?? Do you know how often made a little stone soup eaten two plain [boiled] dumplings, not even a little butter to put on them?? I can't make them [the community] have something to hold over me, they gossip enough already).*

I had heard tales of stone soup over the years but this was my first experience of seeing someone actually boil up a little season to make the neighbours believe they are making soup or stew! Two stones placed in the pot to make it sound like you have soup bones in there. I managed to hold it together until I reached back to the centre where I locked myself in my office and cried like a baby for ages. Miss Fran was even more special to me after that and I made it my business to visit her every day with a little meat-kind to fatten her pot.

Then came the morning a few months later, when I stepped through her gate to see that she had not yet risen, I knew what to expect on opening her door when I saw that her windows were still shut and her step not yet polished. I called out her name knowing inside I would not get an answer. I knocked on her door a couple of times and when silence was my response, I jiggled the handle and opened the door. Miss Fran lay curled up on her bed with her eyes closed, her hands together under her cheek and a smile on her lips, so I knew that whatever her last thoughts and feelings were, they were good. Police were called and she was pronounced dead by the coroner and removed to Maddens, the undertakers. I called one of her 'daughters' on the number Miss Fran had given me for emergencies.

Three weeks later I was invited to speak at her funeral. Seven children that she grew came for the funeral. They came with several nieces and nephews from the U.K., the U.S.A. and Canada. Over the week preceding the funeral, there were nightly 'set ups' with the nine-night (wake) held on the eve of the funeral when a Kumina Band played throughout the night. I listened keenly as her 'children' spoke disparagingly of the one 'son' who, over the years had sent her money. They spoke of how he was still only a shelf packer in a supermarket and lived in a 'government' apartment whilst they, themselves, owned their own homes and had good jobs, one was even a lawyer! Three of them boasted of coming 'home' to Jamaica regularly at least once a year.

Miss Fran was lifted out of a glass carriage and wheeled into the church on Olympic Way in the most ornate casket, decorated with angels and pictures of her. It had a glass top, fancy handles, the works.

The service began, I listened to her 'daughters' eulogising Miss Fran, speaking of how she would hustle all day selling bag juice and sweeties downtown. How she never let them go to bed hungry. How she always found a way to see that they had all they needed for school. How no matter how hard things were, they never missed a day of school. They went on to say how much she had helped them to reach foreign lands and be the successes they had become.

It was now my time to speak, I was shaking uncontrollably, and it wasn't nerves.

"Miss Fran, it saddens my heart to be here today saying goodbye way too soon. How joyful it is to see you sent off in such style, way beyond your expectations, and yet how unnecessary. The cost of one plane ticket would have ensured you were eating properly, or that you never missed a doctor's appointment, or you never missed a medication dose. Your casket could have maintained you medically for several years. This whole funeral package could have fed and sustained you for several more."

"How sad that in the three years I have known you this is the first time that I am meeting your 'children' some of whom, it seems, have visited the Island annually, and yet did not visit you. How sad that you had to die before they came back here, to you. How sad that you struggled so desperately in your final years. How awful that damage done by long-term malnutrition was a contributing factor in your passing. How heart breaking that for all you did for them growing up, they never bothered to check and see that you had what was necessary for you to live beyond existence. How sad that they never witnessed how you proudly boasted of their achievements to all and sundry and what a shame that they never joined you in a pot of 'stone soup'."

"Farewell Miss Fran, until we meet again, sleep on in Jesus' arms."

There was that moment of silence when listeners looked at me open mouthed as if to ask, "Did you really just say that?" the Pastor moved swiftly on to strike up a chorus, 'When the Roll'. You could hear the grumbling over the singing. I'm not one for the graveside so I left after the service,

Of course, there were those who agreed with what I had said and there were those who felt I was the most awful person because I had the temerity to say it like it was. They questioned whether I had seen how many of her family members had attended from foreign and how much they had spent on the set up and funeral for the woman. What they hadn't seen or questioned was the fact that a fraction of what was spent to bury Miss Fran would have allowed her to live, not just barely exist!!!

IRIS

I first met Iris in 2002 when she delivered her nephews to Summer Camp. I say 'delivered' because that is what it looked like, she would bring them to the centre in the churchyard and leave without a word, head down, not engaging with anyone, not even a 'goodbye' to the nephews. On making some enquiries about her, I asked the nephews to get Iris to come see me in the office.

I had learned that Iris had her first baby at just fourteen years old, she hadn't attended school since grade six as she was considered 'slow' and what was the point of spending money to send her to school when she wouldn't or couldn't learn anyway? I had learned that, at nineteen years old, she now had three children, two living with their paternal grandparents and one in state care as she too, has a learning disability.

Iris knocked gently on the open office door, she stood there looking very nervous, unsure if she should come in. I got up and invited her to sit in the chair beside me, hesitatingly she accepted and sat there head down, shoulders hunched and hands wringing in her lap. I sat beside her and asked Iris if she would tell me a bit about the boys who I had nicknamed, 'Trouble' and 'More Trouble', barely eleven months apart in age, they were always into some mischief, like the proverbial 'terrible twins', which they were, for six weeks of the year.

Iris lifted her head and for the first time ever, she looked me in the eye.

"Miss, dem is de debil hisself, two time, memba dat!" *(They are the devil himself, twice, remember that!)*

It was hard not to laugh out loud at the expression on her face, the outright look of pure conviction and warning, paired with the total honesty of a five-year-old. My heart took to her and so began our daily chats, sometimes in the office, often out under the Tamarind trees. Whilst I am by no means an expert in any way, I quickly realised that Iris had the academic level of a six or seven-year-old, but her actions, speech, emotional reactions and most definitely her honest tongue, seemed more that of a younger child. Conversely, she could cuss like any gully queen and move her body like any dancehall queen, in perfect imitation of the women around her who behaved that way.

Over time, through statements like these, I was able to piece together what Iris' life was like.

"From mawnin Miss, mi affi mek ready di boy dem fi mek dem go a school. If dem late mi sista a guh beat mi, nuh dem, an a dem mek wi late" *("From early, Miss, I have to get the boys ready for school. If they're late my sister will beat me, not them and they are why we're late")*

"As mi sista leave guh a work, is den di dutty man cum, wanna deal wid mi. Dem jus hol mi dung an a do dem ting, from mi stop guh a school, true, true, Miss" *(As my sister leaves for work, the dirty men come wanting to have sex. They just hold me down and do what they want, since I stopped going to school, honestly, honestly, Miss)*

I knew I had to be careful how I approached things with her sister as by all accounts she could be quite violent and as is common, she blamed Iris for being 'loose', she blamed Iris for being a victim of repeated rape and abuse.

I went to see Iris at 'home' at a time I knew her sister would be there. I asked if Iris could be available during the day to help me out at the centre.

It was agreed that as long as she didn't fall behind in her chores at home, Iris could come and help out. Iris's face lit up when she realised she would no longer be at home alone during the day and she had a 'job'.

Over the next year, Iris was like my shadow, she and one of my babies, 'Shaday' would argue over who was closest. Between the two, my days were full of laughter.

At the end of the summer I noticed that Iris was becoming a little more distant and yet, more and more reluctant to go home at the end of the day, this indicated to me that her problem was with home and not the centre. I tried to get her to talk about whatever was upsetting her, Iris would just shrug it off and say she was good.

Iris came in and sat with me in the office, she looked totally drawn and stressed, again I asked her what was wrong. All she would say is, "Mi nuh fi tell yuh" and then she began talking about her 'real' babies. That did not sit well with me. I made a note to go down to her lane and do a little detective work the following day.

Iris and I walked towards her lane on my way home, at the top of the lane she turned and gave me a really tight hug and planted a big kiss on my cheek. "Mi luv unnu, yuh cum like mi madda." *("I love you, you seem like my mother".)* Smiling I walked away, maybe she was handling whatever was wrong, she seemed a little more upbeat. I still planned to do my detective work the following day.

My phone was ringing, eleven at night and my phone was ringing, six missed calls from Iris's sister so I called her back.

"Miss Myra, wha mi fi seh, shi gaan, shi gaan." *(Miss Myra, what can I say, she's gone, she's gone.")*

"What she's not home? She run away?"

"No ma'am, is ded shi ded". *(No ma'am, she's dead".)*

"Stop lie!" was my immediate response.

"What happened, who killed her?", I could only think she had been murdered.

I sat in tears trying to take in what was being said to me. My heart was breaking, it was totally shredded by the time I put the phone down.

Iris had been pregnant again. She had gone to a woman outside the community who tried to perform an abortion and in doing so ruptured Iris's womb. She bled to death while being treated at Kington Public Hospital (KPH). No further enquiries appear to have been made as to who performed the botched abortion and the local 'opinion' alternated between blaming Iris for going to 'dash weh' *(abort)* the baby, calling her a 'skettel' *('whore')* and much more. At no time did I hear any condemnation for the men and boys of the community that would rape her on a regular basis. Iris was considered of little worth by anyone because she had a learning disability, she was considered no loss.

I learned over the years that hers was the life of too many women and girls with disabilities living in the communities, especially if they had lost their primary care giver (usually mother or grandmother), or their care giver was aged.

I finally understood why so many disabled children were abandoned to the state, their mothers feeling they would be safer.

One day I hope to open a safe space for girls like Iris, who can live independently some support.

MS MARVA

Ms Marva was the mother of one of our first bursary awardees, Kimberly. She was also one of our first home care workers, a role she fulfilled with joy, passion and compassion. In her early forties, Marva was the mother of three, an adult son, Kimberly and a younger boy. She never took her common entrance exam or went high school as her birth had not been registered and she therefore lacked a birth certificate, vital for registration for the exam and any further schooling. This did not deter Marva from reading all the material she had access to and learning all she could from what was available.

A tall, solid looking woman, Marva commanded the acknowledgement and respect of others with the ease of a natural leader. Unafraid to address any issue and seek solutions, she made the perfect candidate for managing the elders' home and daycare activities and running the programs.

News of the grant from the British Foreign and Commonwealth Office (FCO) coincided with an invitation from Dr. Eldermire-Shearer to send someone from the programme to do the "Care in the Community for the Elderly" six-month postgraduate course she had established at the University of the West Indies. I was amazed at the invitation and even more so at her offer of a fifty per cent discount in the course fees. I needed to find fifty thousand Jamaican dollars which I was able to raise from the training budget within the FCO grant. Now I just had to find the right candidate.

I took Marva out for lunch, away from the community so we could talk, as I felt she would fit the bill. As we ate, we discussed her aspirations and ambition and I told Marva of the offer from the University. It was then that she let me know she never even went to High School, much less possess a University degree. She described how, as an adult, she found the necessary information and registered her own birth. A process that, as a young single mother, took a number of years and all her spare cash, her first child's birth was registered before her own.

I was now in a quandary as to what to do. Over the last year and change I had observed Marva's execution of her duties, she was punctual, polite, enthusiastic, passionate about the elders she cared for and compassionate in her dealings with them. The elders all loved her and she went above and beyond in helping them improve their physical, mental and emotional wellbeing, not officially part of her job, but she saw the needs and responded. She was meticulous in her record keeping, not just noting duties performed and blood pressure, but little things like "Mr. Noisy, looks a bit down, says he's okay, but will drop by later to check", and she would. How could she not be the right candidate?

The only other possible candidate, who in fairness to her, was better educated, had her CXC's and held certification as a Practical Nurse, was better qualified academically. But, oh her attitude, professional for the most part, but very coldly so. Neither she nor the elders seemed to enjoy their time together, there was no real connection and whilst she possessed the passion on occasion, there was no compassion in her dealings with them.

I went to talk to Dr Eldermire-Shearer, told her of my dilemma and said I would be guided by her choice. She listened attentively to the pros and cons of each of the two possible candidates. She asked me if I felt Marva could cope with the academic side of the course, I told I honestly had no idea, but I had witnessed her determination to learn, even without certification. I had observed her dedication both on and off duty, her interactions and attitude towards the elders and more importantly, their attitudes towards her. I watched their faces light up when Ms Marva came to visit or they came to the centre and saw her, I watched them listen attentively as she gave advice on diet, exercise, healthier living and I watched as they carried out her advice and followed her exercise regimes.

I presented the notes of several of the elders which contained the comments of both possible candidates and watched Dr. Eldermire-Shearer smile at what I knew were Marva's comments. She agreed with me, Marva was the right candidate. We were proven right.

Marva came to see me after her first day at UWI, bursting with joy. She told me that the morning was spent getting to know one another and they each student had to introduce themselves and say why they wanted to do the course. Marva shared how as a child, she and her cousins would come up to the University campus to pick mangos. She told them how she had sat up in the trees, admiring the students as they moved around the halls of learning, never dreaming that one day, she too would attend. She said she wanted to complete the course so that she could better serve the elders in the community, helping them to achieve and maintain better health. This had most of her batch-mates crying, all promising to extend any help they could to assist her achieving her goals. They were all professional specialist nurses and social-workers, from all across the Caribbean, Marva was the only non-degree holding participant on the course. She passed out fifth in the class of thirty-four students and earned the admiration of all her batch-mates and tutors.

When the FCO funding ceased, Marva went on to work at the infirmary at St Joseph's in Kingston later becoming a ward manager and she still, to this day, looks out for the elders in the community.

FROM GARRISON TO GARDEN VOL. 2 - TIME FOR SANCTUARY

Chapter 1

TIME TO MOVE

It was September and I was looking forward to going home to spend some time with my family. Summer Camp was over and whilst things were fairly quiet between the communities, there were the odd intra-community spats, usually at night.

I headed to Phillipo Avenue from Tower Avenue, along Olympic Way as the short cut across Raniford's bushy wasteland, was a bit dodgy. I had the one working laptop over a very weary shoulder, it had been a long day.

I turned off Olympic Way, stopped to buy some juice by Ms Mitzie on Delisser Avenue and moved onto Richard Hill Road. Halfway down, there was a barrage of gunshot behind me and with that, every gate on Richard Hill slammed shut, grills locked in great haste. I looked in front and behind me, there was nowhere to go, nowhere to duck or hide. I had neither the energy to climb over a fence (to possibly face bad dogs), nor the energy to run. I prayed, I prayed for strength and for protection, shrugged my shoulders and continued toward the house, trusting in my prayer.

I sat down on my bed and shook when I realised the bullet that slammed into the wooden light post across the road as I walked down Richard Hill, could easily have come down the side of the road I was walking on or had the post been concrete, ricocheted and hit me. A tad too close for comfort, again, definitely time to move from within the community.

The house-hunting began and within the week I was blessed in being offered a lovely two-bedroom house on a scheme outside Spanish Town, Angels Two at a reasonable rent. I only had a bed and mattress, the house came with a stove and fridge, I had the basic necessities and I no longer had the nightly lullaby of gunshot.

The lovely Linda Lane from the British High Commission came to visit and a few days later appeared with two big white wicker baskets containing, crockery, cutlery, pots and pans, she also brought a chest of drawers, a huge pair of floor cushions, two reclining garden chairs with pads, a bunch of scatter cushions and a garden table with four matching chairs. I was now fully furnished and I was now a commuter.

Travelling in and out of Kingston was pretty simple, if I was ready to leave by five-thirty a.m., there was an executive bus that picked up literally, outside my gate, otherwise I would take a fifty-dollar route taxi to Spanish Town from outside the Angels Plaza, a three-minute walk from the house. From Spanish Town it was a JUTC (Jamaica Urban Transport Company, Government) bus to Three Miles then route taxi or bus down Olympic Way to Tower Avenue, all in little over an hour door to door, usually. The journey at the end of the day was very different, if I hadn't left the centre by 4p.m. in order to be in and out of Spanish Town before dark, I would wait until it was dark and charter a trusted taxi from within the community. I also used this mode of travel when broke, as the taxi drivers trusted me to pay as soon as I was again in pocket, not a courtesy I could expect from the buses. So, know that if I was seen in a taxi during the day, it was because I was broke and didn't even have bus fare.

I enjoyed my morning bus ride into 'Town', there was always something going on to amuse, entertain or educate and if I caught the right number 22 bus, would get a short verse from the bible, a quick prayer, followed by sweet gospel songs sung by an amazing elder church 'mother', with the most melodic voice, Mother P. Although her clothes were obviously fairly worn, they were impeccably clean, well pressed and any holes, darned or patched. Her shoes, however down at heel, always shone with a military gleam. Her smile was infectious and her eyes shone with a passion for her morning 'service', which was enjoyed by most on board. There were a significant number of us who would wait for 'her' bus, even if it meant arriving late at our destinations.

As I travelled home to London, I had no inclination that Jamaica was about to enter its most murderous period with one thousand, six hundred and seventy-four people dead, sixty-three I personally knew, some on just a nodding basis, others, I had reasoned with daily.

2005 was going to prove to be extremely challenging.

ABOUT THE AUTHOR

Moira Morgan

Moira was born in 1954 in Dublin to a large, strong, Irish Catholic family, where service to others was the order of the day.

She is mother of four, grandmother of ten, 'foster' mum to many more over the years.

Using her life experiences and administrative skills gained over many genres, she spent close to twenty years, spanning three decades, volunteering in some of Jamaica's most challenged and challenging inner city communities.

Contact: momorganbooks@gmail.com

PRAISE FOR AUTHOR

" This book chronicles the author's journey, one may say love relationship, with Jamaica. It is well written, easy to follow; with emotional highs and lows, told as if it were an unfolding story. "
Dr Henley Morgan – Community Activist - Trenchtown - Kingston Jamaica

"A truly fascinating book. It reads very well and I went through every emotion known to a human being, from laughter, anger, sadness, shock/disbelief, disgust. What pathos as the writer brought how she felt real for the reader. That is exactly how one should write a book of their real- life experience.
 The tears I shed as a grown man were real, Stone Soup, Iris and Marva had me crying for the longest while. This book has impacted me in a huge way. I am so glad that I had the opportunity to work on such a touching experience as it has left an indelible mark on me. Can't wait for the next book."
Tony Kelly - (Editor) Retired Teacher and Social Worker, Community Activist - Birmingham UK

"I found this book to be thoroughly readable and indeed enjoyable, very very funny in some parts, very sad in others. The author has really lived inner city life to the hilt, described it vividly and accurately, I rate her highly for that. No wonder that young and old all loved her. Colour and origin are no barriers to our 'ordinary' people, the poor who know God way before the rest of us and know how to recognise love and goodness when they see it regardless of appearances. So, they took her in.

As an account of inner city life this book has much in common with Angela Stultz's, Signs and Wonders, since they are both writing about the warring groups and getting them to make peace. The differences lie in their diverse origins (Irish Catholic and Black Rasta), sources of funding and 'institutions', and the resulting emphases – Angela's more developmental, the writer's more welfare, though the line between these two are more fluid that those words and categories might suggest."

Horace Levy - Retired Senior Lecturer Department of Sociology and Social Work, University of the West Ondies, Mona Campus Jamaica, Human Rights Activist

"Failure to listen to the cries of the voices documented in these pages by this daughter of the soil, can only be to the peril of this beautiful vibrant society, a place which a couple millions of us, lovingly and unrepentantly call home."

Claudette Carwford Brown Phd, Child and Family Welfare Consultant. Senior Lecturer in Climical Social Work, Univertsity of the West Indies, Mona Campus, Jamaica.

FROM GARRISON TO GARDEN

From Garrison to Garden charts the twenty year journey, across three decades, through some of Jamaica's most challenging and challenged inner city Kingston communities, telling the untold stories along the way.

From Garrison To Garden - Vol 1 - Boots On The Ground

Boots on the Ground takes you through the first trips to Jamaica, from the first family trip in 1977, through to the summer of 2004. In doing so charts the progress from first trip, through visists, to the initiation and implementation of community owned development programmes that have changed lives and the commnunities they serve, telling the stories of real people.

From Garrison To Garden - Vol 2 - Time For Sactuary

Time for Sanctuary takes us through from Summer Camp 2004 which brought in volunteers from across the UK to set up Summer Camp and train community youth to take over after they left to British High Commission pool trips, Hurricane Ivan, to the initiation and implementation of the "Hush the Guns" and "Springboard" prison rehabilitation programmes. 2004 to 2009. encompassing the establishment of the Sanctuary, an inntergenerational safe space for elders and children.

From Garrison To Garden - Vol 3 - Journey To The Oasis

2010 to date. The journey to our permanent home in St Thomas. The Tivoli incursion 2010, the repercussions in the varuious communities. Search for a permanent home, where we are at today.

Printed in Poland
by Amazon Fulfillment
Poland Sp. z o.o., Wrocław

60823819R00094